LEARNING
WORDS

INSIDE & OUT

LEARNING WORDS

INSIDE & OUT

Vocabulary Instruction That Boosts Achievement in All Subject Areas

NANCY FREY & DOUGLAS FISHER

Foreword by DONNA OGLE

HEINEMANN
PORTSMOUTH, NH

Heinemann
361 Hanover Street
Portsmouth, NH 03801–3912
www.heinemann.com

Offices and agents throughout the world

The authors and publisher wish to thank those who have generously given permission to reprint borrowed material:

Cover image from *The Giant of Seville* by Dan Andreasen. Copyright © 2007 by Dan Andreasen. Published by Abrams Books for Young Readers. Reprinted by permission of Harry N. Abrams, Inc.

Cover image from *The Great American Mousical* by Julie Andrews Edwards. Text copyright © 2006 by Julie Andrews Edwards. Jacket art copyright © 2006 by Tony Walton. Used by permission of HarperCollins Publishers.

(*continued on page 183*)

Library of Congress Cataloging-in-Publication Data
Frey, Nancy.
  Learning words inside and out, grades 1–6 : vocabulary instruction that boosts achievement in all subject areas / Nancy Frey and Douglas Fisher.
       p. cm.
  Includes bibliographical references and index.
  ISBN-13: 978-0-325-02612-1
  ISBN-10: 0-325-02612-2
  1. Vocabulary—Study and teaching (Elementary).   2. Language arts—Correlation with content subjects.   I. Fisher, Douglas.   II. Title.
LB1574.5.F78 2009
372.6'1—dc22   2008044973

Editor: Wendy Murray
Production: Lynne Costa
Cover design: Shawn Girsberger
Interior photographs: Ana Muro, Lauderbach Elementary, Chula Vista, CA
Typesetter: House of Equations, Inc.
Manufacturing: Valerie Cooper

Printed in the United States of America on acid-free paper
13 12 11 10 09   VP   1 2 3 4 5

Contents

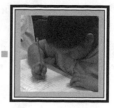

Foreword

Nancy Frey and Doug Fisher have given all elementary teachers a real gift with this guide to teaching and learning subject area (academic) vocabulary. The issues they address reflect their understanding of schools' and teachers' concerns. Their engaging classroom examples confirm that vocabulary learning can be enjoyable when focused on important subject area terms.

Vocabulary instruction is perhaps the most overlooked area of literacy instruction today. Judith Scott, Dianne Jamieson-Noel, and Marlene Asselin (2003) found in their study of upper-elementary classrooms that only 1.4 percent of instructional time in academic areas was devoted to word learning. Frey and Fisher take on this dismal reality and set about developing a strong argument for change. What they have created is an inviting and persuasive guide for elementary teachers to follow to restructure their subject area instruction to include meaningful attention to vocabulary. They address teachers' basic questions clearly and with specific suggestions and supports. The organization of the book is also straightforward and creates an inviting path for teachers to follow.

With my colleagues Camille Blachowicz and Peter Fisher, I have spent a great deal of effort exploring ways to expand teachers' knowledge of and commitment to vocabulary instruction. We know that classrooms in which there is ongoing attention to words and fascination with language provide the foundation for successful vocabulary instruction. In these word-rich classrooms teachers can then address a major challenge and opportunity: attention to academic vocabulary. Technical terms and new uses of familiar words in science, social studies, and math often create stumbling blocks for students who are not word savvy. Yet these challenges also present ongoing opportunities to highlight words, show their relationships, and help students think about words with new intensity. With focused instruction, students can build their word knowledge, learn strategies for determining the meanings of academic terms, and practice using these words frequently in oral and written forms. Content areas are rich sources for word work; words are important and students hear, see, and use the new terms frequently. This makes it more likely that students will appreciate the value of word study.

I agree with Frey and Fisher that the content areas are a great context for vocabulary instruction. With time at a premium, integrating attention to words and word-learning strategies within content concept development makes real sense. This book lays out what teachers need to know to create this kind of rich, intentional instructional program. Frey and Fisher lead teachers step-by-step in developing interesting vocabulary instruction across the subject areas. You will want to use this resource and share it with other teachers.

Donna Ogle
Professor
National-Louis University
Chicago, Illinois

Why Teaching Subject Area Words Can Make or Break Achievement

IT WAS AFTER LUNCH IN MARIO'S THIRD GRADE CLASS and time for social studies. Mario was reading over a worksheet that featured ten vocabulary terms related to geography, including *cardinal directions*, *poles*, *equator*, *geography*, *latitude*, *longitude*, *map key*, *legend*, *hemisphere*, and *compass rose*. His task was to alphabetize the list, write definitions for each word, and then use each in a sentence. Like many of his classmates, Mario spent the next fifteen minutes diligently looking up the words in dictionaries and in the text-book's glossary before cobbling together the definitions. Adapting the first meaning presented in the dictionary for the word *legend*, Mario wrote this definition:

A story from the past

He then wrote a sentence containing the word *legend*:

The legend of the coyote was told by the Native Americans.

Given that much of his experience in third-grade social studies thus far had focused on Native Americans in California, the definition and sentence are reasonable guesses. In addition, he had been reading about legends, fables, and tall tales during the literacy block and especially enjoyed *The Giant of Seville* (Andreasen 2008). Recalling that the "tall tale" in that book turned out to be true, he added another sentence to his worksheet for good measure:

Sometimes a legend is true,
like with the giant named Martin Bates.

Mario slogged through the rest of the task, completing definitions and sentences for the other nine words designed to introduce students to the unit of study. For some of the words you could see Mario understood the topic at hand, while his work on other words displayed that he was not making worthwhile connections between this exercise and the historical context. It's not surprising, then, that the task did not get Mario any closer to mastering the content standards focused on geography. Nor did this vocabulary task prepare him for the reading he was expected to do, the mapping skills he was expected to develop, or the classroom discussions he was expected to participate in. The vocabulary work took class time but did not scaffold his understanding of content in any significant way. Classmates of his who did "better" than him on the task also lost precious class time, for the task didn't deepen their knowledge either.

Quite frankly, we don't have this time to waste on ineffective approaches. Vocabulary development is critical, and yet few teachers feel sure-footed about how to achieve it. It seems as though over the last few years there has been more attention in the field paid to the issue of teaching subject matter vocabulary, yet when we looked to the research base for next steps, we found it has focused on isolated instructional routines and activities. Our motivation for developing this book was to discover what works in improving subject matter vocabulary over the long haul. We wanted to design and implement an intentional vocabulary approach that was part of the

overall classroom experience that students would have, and not simply a series of activities to episodically engage them in word learning.

We are also concerned that despite the evidence that vocabulary learning should occur across subjects, in many elementary classrooms this instruction is relegated to the language arts curriculum. Scott, Jamieson-Noel, and Asselin (2003) reported that only 1.4 percent of instructional time in the elementary content disciplines (math, science, social studies, and the arts) was devoted to word learning. A major purpose of this book is to help you change this statistic in your classroom.

And so we set out to identify effective practices. We tried them out for ourselves, in our own classrooms as well as in the classrooms of our friends and colleagues, to determine how students could be engaged with subject area vocabulary learning. In addition, we have tracked the implementation of these approaches using both quantitative and qualitative measures, to ensure that they are effective (e.g., Fisher and Frey 2007, 2008), so we would feel comfortable making specific recommendations.

With this book, our goal is to show you a teaching and learning framework that helps make students self-regulating, independent word learners.

We want to move your thinking hundreds of miles away from the view of vocabulary instruction as disembodied lists for students to memorize and toward a stance where word learning is fun for students, is an excuse to interact with peers, and gives students the intellectual and social currency of being able to think, speak, read, and write with greater facility.

■ Purposeful Word Learning: Improving Students' Reading, Writing, and Thinking

We've organized the rest of this chapter around the questions that elementary teachers ask us concerning vocabulary learning. We consider what research and our own teaching experience have to offer on these issues, so that we all have in mind the same lay of the land. Then, in each of the following chapters, we focus on one facet of vocabulary development. Taken together, these facets provide you with an *intentional vocabulary initiative* that can transform students of all abilities into proficient readers, because they bring to texts banks of word knowledge that help them access the language of ideas. Students become proficient writers, too, for their vocabularies help them say what they mean—and convey what they know.

What Are the Benefits of Spending Time on Vocabulary Instruction?

Teachers see evidence of the need for vocabulary instruction each time they sit down with a guided reading group: without vocabulary knowledge, the reading material at hand is incomprehensible. Young readers in particular come with a wide range of language experiences, so vocabulary knowledge cannot be assumed. One child may have spent hours in the natural history museum gazing at dinosaurs, while the child next to her may know about dinosaurs only from reruns of *The Flintstones*. Which child is likely to comprehend the reading on *Tyrannosaurus rex*?

Teachers juggle math, science, social studies, reading and language arts, as well as the visual and performing arts. In addition, there is the constant pressure of standardized testing performance. You're right to wonder, *What can I leave out? I don't have enough time as it is!* If you're covering vocabulary and not seeing the results you'd like, it is reasonable to think it's a losing battle to pour more time into vocabulary instruction. After all, you can't run off to the natural history museum to catch up the ones who haven't had those prior language experiences.

But here's the thing: vocabulary is among the greatest predictors of reading comprehension (Baker, Simmons, and Kame'enui 1998), and reading

A guided reading group

comprehension, it almost goes without saying, is central to learning in the content areas. The relationship between vocabulary and reading proficiency is so powerful that there is evidence that vocabulary size in kindergarten is an effective predictor of reading comprehension and academic achievement in the later school years (Scarborough 2001).

If you doubt this, consider the fact that missing just 5 percent of the words makes a text nearly incomprehensible. Five percent doesn't sound like a lot, but try to read the passage in Figure 1.1, in which we have removed 5 percent of the text and replaced it with nonsense words. You may glean that the text is about coffee, but you'd have a hard time answering questions about the text, right? In this case, you probably have significant background knowledge that you can use to fill in the gaps in your word knowledge. Imagine if you had limited background knowledge about the topic and didn't know the words. The text would become incomprehensible.

Now consider the role that vocabulary plays in writing proficiency. We know that writing is thinking. (Have you ever tried to write and not think? Impossible.) So, how does a writer think? He thinks in language, in words.

Factoid 1

Caffeine is tasteless. A "strong" wepuha is mostly the result of the amount of coffee in relation to the amount of water. The longer a bean is sisku, the less caffeine it has. "Arabica" beans have less caffeine than "Robusta" beans. "Arabica" beans have more flavor than "Robusta" beans, which are mostly used in high-volume coffees and instant coffees.

Factoid 2

Wepuha is the way the bean is edusca, not the bean itself. You can use many different balksiks to produce wepuha coffee. You can also use the wepuha roasted coffee to make a larger cup of coffee. In the United States, wepuha roasting results mostly in a darker roast than wepuha roasting in Europe.

Figure 1.1 *Checking comprehension when 5 percent of the words are unknown*

In general, the more words a person knows, the better he is at writing. And the better he is at writing, the better he is at thinking. We know that this sounds like circular logic, but we think of it as recursive and interconnected. As students learn, they acquire labels for ideas. As they think, they can use those labels. As they write, they clarify their understanding of those ideas and even generate new understandings. Writing is evidence of the incorporation of information. Extensive vocabularies help one refine one's thinking through more nuance and sophistication. Word knowledge, in a sense, makes us smarter. Suffice it to say that vocabulary instruction improves writing (Cantrell 1999; Stevens 2006).

What Does It Mean to Know a Word?

You ask the students in your first-grade class about the meaning of the word *triangle* and get a range of answers. Some make a triangle shape with their fingers, while others might point to a triangle shape posted on the wall. One student says that a triangle is a musical instrument. A few are able to tell you that it is a shape with three sides. How would you describe their knowledge of this term?

What does it mean to know a word? Is it to recognize it? To be able to define it? To use it correctly—in all of its shades of meaning—in our verbal and written language? Consider the word *provocative*. You've heard it and no doubt used it. But think about the depth of word knowledge required to use this word well. As a case in point, an editor wrote in the margin of our book draft, "This is quite provocative!" We knew she meant challenging, thought provoking, not that our statement about reading aloud was the stuff of a romance novel. But would the average student be able to tease out the appropriate meaning from context? Wise word users have a depth of knowledge.

Beck and her colleagues (2002) get at this idea of depth by distinguishing between shallow and deep word knowledge. By shallow word knowledge, they mean that students memorize definitions and do not have the deeper knowledge of the concepts that the words represent. To extend their metaphor, the range of people's word knowledge is like the difference between the shallow end of a swimming pool, the deep end, and the deep blue sea (in the case of linguists who know several languages or those well versed in word histories). While our students might not reach the deep-sea levels of professional linguists, our goal as teachers ought to be that they are able to know words deeply enough that they can use them flexibly across content areas, something we look at in more detail in later chapters.

So, depth matters. That is, knowing the multiple meanings of words matters, and reasoning a word's meaning in context matters. This view of vocabulary is relatively new. Vocabulary knowledge studies from the 1940s and 1950s focused on recall and recognition, usually through one-trial learning, followed by a quiz asking participants to list words when given the meaning (recall) or to identify the correct word on a multiple-choice test (recognition). Researchers soon saw the limitations of this kind of contrived measurement, especially because it did not reflect the ways in which vocabulary knowledge is authentically used. (But you can see how this recall-and-recognition approach continues to dig its claws into instructional ideas.) Measurement of vocabulary knowledge was refined to assess five dimensions (Cronbach 1942, cited in Graves 1986):

- *generalization* through definitional knowledge
- *application* through correct usage
- *breadth* through recall of words
- *precision* through understanding of examples and nonexamples
- *availability* through use of vocabulary in discussion

Dale, O'Rourke, and Baumann (1971) further refined our concept of vocabulary knowledge by noting that words do not simply fall into two categories, known and unknown. Instead, they suggested that there are degrees of knowing a word. Their continuum consists of four stages:

1. having never seen or heard the word;
2. having heard the word, but not knowing what it means;

3. recognizing the word in context; and

4. knowing and using the word.

The problem with the vocabulary worksheet Mario and his classmates were given was that it didn't really measure the depth of students' word knowledge across these four phases. Mario had shallow word knowledge, and the poorly designed worksheet task allowed him to go down the wrong garden path—that is, work with the wrong word meaning—without realizing it. If Mario had gone into the task with a deep knowledge of the word *legend*, he might have written something like "The legend of a map helps us understand scale and symbols." A stronger vocabulary activity would have scaffolded students' understanding more, guiding Mario and his classmates to consider context when choosing between the meanings of *legend* as a story passed down through generations and as a guide useful for map reading.

Focus on English Language Learners

Children who are learning English are especially vexed by multiple-meaning words. Even as they acquire a new language, they might be limited to a single meaning of a word. Anticipate possible areas of confusion and provide an explanation of new word knowledge. When applicable, link it to previous knowledge, and give written examples of multiple-meaning words using simple graphic organizers.

How Do I Get My Students to Own Their Word Learning?

In too many classrooms, we see teachers working hard to teach vocabulary, only to have it fade away as soon as the next unit begins. For example, there's lots of effort to make sure that students understand terms like *heat* and *temperature* during a science unit on the solar system; however, a few weeks later, these terms seem to disappear from students' vocabulary when they begin working in the unit on energy. We were in a classroom one day when a student indignantly told his teacher, "I thought we only needed to know that for the sun test!"

At some point, it would seem that students must move from merely learning words to learning *about* their own learning of words. The role of metacognitive awareness in the learning lives of students is critical in their continued development as self-regulated learners. The National Research Council (1999) has had quite a bit to say about this. It defines *metacognition* as "people's ability to predict their performances on various tasks . . . and to monitor their current levels of mastery and understanding" (12). Learning, after all, isn't just about being able to recall information; it is a process enacted upon by the learner. When you hear talk about "active learning," you're hearing the rumble of metacognition. A goal of teaching for metacognitive awareness is that students develop an adaptive expertise so that they can apply what they know flexibly and use what they know to learn new skills—analogous to the difference between being able to follow a recipe and creating a new one (Hatano and Ignaki 1986).

Now think about this: When was the last time you acquired new vocabulary by writing a list and then memorizing it? Let's say you bought a new hybrid phone and dove into the instruction manual so you could operate it. Undoubtedly you encountered words you knew (*phone, camera, address book*), words you partially knew (*multiconnector, messaging button*), and terms that were completely foreign to you (*SIM card, Bluetooth*). First, you noticed what you knew and didn't know (monitoring). Then you set about learning the terms because you recognized that you couldn't understand the manual without knowing these words. You looked at the diagrams and compared them with your phone. You checked the back for a glossary. You may have even enlisted the help of a tech-savvy teenager to give you a hand. The point is, you could predict the likelihood of your success with the task, you knew you needed to master the vocabulary, and you knew how to help yourself learn it. That's metacognition at work.

Similarly, students need to be taught metacognitively as they acquire vocabulary knowledge. Teachers model their own thinking as they encounter words in text that might be confusing and show students how they figure out those terms. As we will also see, students need rich oral language experiences that cause them to utilize new vocabulary in discussion and clarify and refine their understanding of words with peers. They also need to learn strategies for helping themselves when reading independently, especially in getting unstuck when they encounter a tricky term. Ultimately, subject area word learning is as much about problem solving as it is about acquisition.

How Many Words Do Students Need to Learn?

One of the most common questions teachers ask concerns the number of words that students need to know to be successful. Nagy and Anderson (1984) noted that students would come in contact with 88,500 word families by the time they entered high school. Word families are groups of words consisting of the same root or base and their associated compounds and derivates.

These 88,500 word families translate to about 500,000 individual words. Thankfully for readers and their teachers, about half of these word families are used so rarely that students will likely encounter them just once in a lifetime. (It's unlikely that you will ever need to know that *blepharospasm* is an involuntary twitching of an eyelid, unless you are an ophthalmologist.) Even reducing the number of word families and words a student needs to know by half is overwhelming, especially if you think that you have to directly teach all of these words! If a student needs to know 250,000 words and has 180 days of school for thirteen years, that student will have to learn 107 words per day and never be absent. As we will see throughout this book, students learn a lot of these words while reading. Other words must be explicitly, systematically, and intentionally taught. They key to improving student achievement is knowing the difference between words students will learn automatically and words they will need to be taught.

Word wall of content area words

Which Words Should I Teach?

Over the past decade, a great deal of agreement has been reached about vocabulary instruction. In general, experts agree that there are three types of words that students need to know. Beck, McKeown, and Kucan (2002) identify these as Tier 1, Tier 2, and Tier 3 words. Others, such as Vacca and Vacca (2007), identify these words as general, specialized, and technical. If Mario's teacher had used this classification system, the words she selected might appear in the categories identified in Figure 1.2. We consider each of these classifications in this chapter and then use this information to select words for systemic instruction in Chapter 2.

General Vocabulary

By Tier 1 or general vocabulary, these researchers mean words that are basic for reading. These words are typically in the spoken vocabulary of most students and rarely need to be taught. Unfortunately, in many classrooms instructional time is wasted on explicit instruction for words students will learn in other ways. These words develop as students read and are read to (see Chapter 6 for more information about this process). General vocabulary words are not conceptually difficult, either, and are especially appropriate for learning through wide reading.

Specialized Vocabulary

Tier 2 or specialized words are those high-utility terms that often change meaning in different contexts. They are the words that confuse most readers

General (Tier 1) Words	Specialized (Tier 2) Words	Technical (Tier 3) Words
Area	Elevation	Cardinal direction
Direction	Globe	Compass rose
Distance	Hemisphere	Continent
East	Legend	Equator
Land	Position	Geography
Location	Region	Latitude
Map		Longitude
North		Map grid
Place		Map key
South		Meridian
West		

Figure 1.2 *Vocabulary words for geography unit separated by category*

and are significantly undertaught in most classrooms. This category also includes words for which students know some part of the meaning, but do not have mastery of the complexity of the words' meaning. These words are critical for understanding. Imagine the student who is working with the word *expression* as it relates to a character's expression in a piece of fiction. Later that day, the student might be expected to write an expression during math. Mario's teacher acknowledged that these words were critical for understanding the content but failed to recognize the effect that multiple meanings and context have on words such as *legend, hemisphere,* and *cardinal.*

As another example of the power of these specialized words, read the following sentence from a sixth-grade textbook:

> Catherine the Great, a minor aristocrat from Germany, became Empress of Russia when her husband Peter, the grandson of Peter the Great, was killed.

The specialized word in this sentence is *minor*. To test our hypothesis that students use context in determining word meaning, we asked one hundred fourth graders, one hundred seventh graders, and one hundred tenth graders what *minor* meant in this sentence. On a multiple-choice test, the majority of fourth graders indicated that Catherine the Great was "digging for gold" when she met her husband. Interestingly, the majority of seventh graders got the question right, selecting the response that she "wasn't very important." The highest percentage of incorrect answers came from the tenth graders (70 percent), who most often selected the choice that Catherine the Great was "underage when she married Peter."

Again, context matters. Students use what they know and are familiar with to determine word meanings. In California, fourth graders study the Gold Rush and in tenth grade students think about their age all of the time as they wait to drive, vote, and legally enter a bar. To ensure their understanding of this text, the teacher would have to attend to the word *minor* by providing students multiple opportunities to use this specialized term in different contexts. This might occur through word sorts, word maps, or writing tasks.

Tier 3 or technical words are those that are bound to a specific discipline. These are the seductive content words that teachers love to focus upon: *ecology, pointillism, hieroglyphic, vowel, parallelogram,* and so on. Sometimes these words need to be directly taught and other times they simply need to be defined. The decision to teach the word versus explain the word should be based on the future utility of the word and its relative importance in facilitating or blocking understanding. Again, conceptual difficulty plays a role in what gets taught and how. The term *parallelogram* represents an intricate knowledge set in mathematics and defies simple definitional instruction, especially because of its contrastive concepts, *quadrilateral* and *rhombus*. (You may recall from your own math classes that a parallelogram is a quadrilateral with parallel opposite sides, and a rhombus is a quadrilateral with equal sides.) By contrast, it is possible to teach *pointillism* through definition—it is a painting method that uses very small colored dots to create a larger image. There are deeper layers to pointillism: it uses primary colors to fool the eye into believing there are secondary colors, and George Seurat is a major artist associated with the technique. However, goals of recall, recognition, application, and precision influence the time an art teacher will spend on instruction. Most obviously, the important words to teach are those that are critical for understanding the text or the content.

For example, while reading aloud *The Great American Mousical* (Edwards and Hamilton 2006), Ms. Ruiz chose to explain the word *metropolis* and

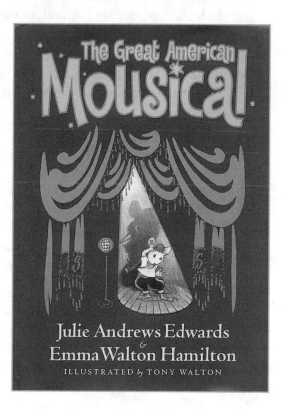

not spend extended time on teaching it. The passage that opens the book reads:

> If you could stand upon a faraway star and look down on planet Earth on a cloudless evening, you might just notice a glowing pool of light . . . and chances are, that glow would be New York City. If you could leap from your star and fly down, down, down into the heart of that great metropolis, you would land in the most twinkling, sparkling place of all—Times Square. (1)

Ms. Ruiz was more interested in the story that Julie Andrews and her daughter had to tell and knew that she would teach the words from the book that related to drama such as *scenery, balcony, orchestra pit, boxed sections, proscenium,* and *apron of the stage.* These words were consistent with the visual and performing arts standards Ms. Ruiz wanted to teach and were words that students of drama should know. In other words, they are the technical words that help define the discipline.

■ Intentional Vocabulary Instruction

Sadly, vocabulary instruction in many classrooms is often neglected or occurs in ineffective, or even harmful, ways. To change this and increase the quality of vocabulary instruction requires a sustained focus on content area vocabulary. Teachers have to teach students *how* to learn new words, not just the meanings of specific words. If word learning occurred only through direct instruction, as some researchers recommend, then teachers would have to spend every minute of every day getting students to learn their daily 107 words. In contrast, we think that students should be taught how to learn words through wide reading, teacher modeling, *and* explicit, systematic, and intentional instruction.

We have developed a subject area vocabulary initiative that consists of five big ideas. Each of the five big ideas is further developed in the chapters that follow. Taken together, this approach serves to develop the general, specialized, and technical vocabulary necessary for student success, both inside and outside of school. For now, let's briefly explore each of the big ideas.

1. *Make It Intentional.* First and foremost, we have to intentionally select words that are worth teaching. We need to carefully consider the types of words students need to know and learn. Students need to understand technical words to become proficient with the discourse of the discipline. They also need to know the specialized words that are commonly used but that change their meaning based on the context or content area in which they are used. The key here is to determine which words students need to know and how to best teach them. Accordingly, in Chapter 2, we focus on an instructional design model that is intentional and takes into account what is known about human learning. Our intentional vocabulary learning model is based on a gradual release of responsibility of learning theory, which suggests that teachers should purposefully plan to increase student responsibility for learning.

2. *Make It Transparent.* One way that students learn is through teacher modeling. The purpose of this component of subject area vocabulary instruction is twofold. The first is to develop what Michael Graves (2006) calls "word consciousness" by drawing attention to the language used by the writer. The second is to teach procedures for problem solving unknown or poorly understood words. It is also important to discriminate between these two purposes and teaching specific vocabulary words. It seems reasonable to suggest that modeling word-solving strategies and word-learning strategies across content areas will help students learn words by providing them with cognitive guidance and a how-to model. However, using teacher modeling to teach individual words out of context is an inefficient use of instructional time. When teachers read aloud to their students and share their thinking about the words in the text, they develop their students' metacognitive skills.

3. *Make It Useable.* While we know that modeling is critical for student success, we also understand that immediately after this modeling, students have to use the words they've been taught if they are to own them. Students simply will not incorporate content area vocabulary into their speaking and writing unless they are provided multiple opportunities to do so. Collaborative tasks that require students to use newly acquired vocabulary verbally or in writing are thus a part of our model. Authentic usage is essential for acquisition of vocabulary knowledge.

4. *Make It Personal.* Independent learning is a vital but often undervalued aspect of word acquisition. In this strand of our model, students are given tasks that allow them to apply what they have learned in novel situations. This component is critical if students are to move beyond passive participants and incorporate new subject matter word learning into their funds of knowledge. Students have an opportunity to take ownership of the vocabulary by integrating it into their personal verbal and written repertoires.

5. *Make It a Priority.* We know that reading has an impact on vocabulary. As such, students must be engaged in authentic reading tasks, reading texts they can read, on a daily basis. The best way to do this is to ensure that the school places a high priority on wide reading. In reading widely, students acquire some of the general words they need to know. In addition, they see familiar words in diverse contexts and add new meanings to known words. In addition to wide reading, another schoolwide component of our subject area vocabulary approach encourages all teachers to focus on high-frequency prefix, suffix, and root words. In focusing on these words, students develop transportable skills in making educated guesses about words they do not know. As we will see in Chapter 6, there are clusters of words that share meanings, and studying them together helps students remember them.

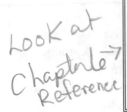
Look at Chapter 6 Reference →

What Could Mario Do Had This Been His Experience?

Remember Mario's vocabulary task? Let's reengineer his learning through the lens of systematic, explicit, and intentional content area word learning. First, he would have read about the use of geography and map skills in class and at home. Doing so would have built his background knowledge and vocabulary. A list of sample books representing a range of difficulty levels can be found in Figure 1.3.

At the same time, his teacher would have read aloud to the class and explained her thinking as she did so. She would have solved unknown words during her readings and modeled for students how they might figure out an unknown word. For example, had she read *Geography from A to Z: A Picture Glossary* (Knowlton 1997), she could have shared her thinking about some of the terms introduced in the book. She also could have projected a map from the Internet (see, for example, www.nationalgeographic.com/resources/ngo/maps) and explained her understanding of each of the terms on the map, including *legend*. She would have described her experiences with maps, both positive and negative. She might even have taught the

---

Aberg, R. 2003. *Latitude and Longitude*. New York: Children's Press.

Cummings, P., and L. Cummings. 1998. *Talking with Adventurers*. Washington, DC: National Geographic.

Layne, S. L. 1998. *Thomas's Sheep and the Great Geography Test*. Gretna, LA: Pelican.

Parsons, J. 2006. *Geography of the World*. New York: Dorling Kindersley.

Petty, K. 2000. *The Amazing Pop-Up Geography Book*. New York: Dutton.

Shulevitz, U. 2008. *How I Learned Geography*. New York: Farrar, Straus, and Giroux.

Wade, M. D. 2003. *Types of Maps*. New York: Children's Press.

Figure 1.3 *Diverse books about geography*

students "The Longitude/Latitude Rap," by Ron Brown, found at http://songsforteaching.com/geography/longitudelatitudemapreading.htm.

In addition, Mario's teacher would have focused instruction on the specialized and technical words she selected. As is further explored in Chapters 4 and 5, she could have used semantic feature analysis, concept maps, text impressions, or vocabulary cards. For instance, she could have created a word map with the class on the word *equator*, like the one in Figure 1.4.

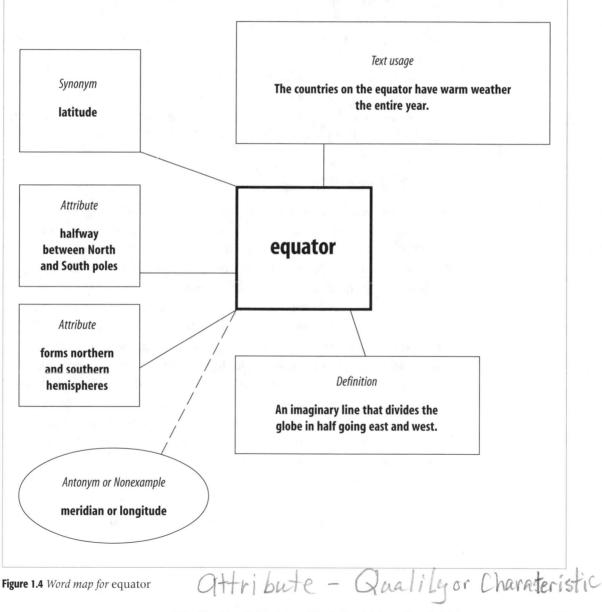

Figure 1.4 *Word map for* equator

Why Teaching Subject Area Words Can Make or Break Achievement ■ ■ ■ **17**

And finally (if he had been lucky), Mario would have been exposed to a number of prefixes, suffixes, and roots that would relate to the words under investigation. His teacher could have shown her students that *hemisphere* contains the prefix *hemi-*, meaning half. Or she might have explained that the word *geography* itself contains the prefix *geo-* from the Greek word for earth, which generally means ground or land, and *graphy*, which means writing or the study of a written form of knowledge.

Taken together, this intentional approach to vocabulary development would have strengthened Mario's vocabulary knowledge inside and out of this content area. In addition, he would have developed a deeper conceptual and definitional understanding of the words in the unit, having learned a number of words inside and out. He would also know how to figure out unknown words because his teacher would have modeled looking inside and outside of specific words to determine word meanings. And finally, Mario would have been more likely to apply the words correctly in his own speaking and writing, both inside and outside the school building.

■ The Takeaway

Without question, vocabulary knowledge is critical. Knowledge of and about words not only serves as an excellent predictor of students' achievement but is inexorably linked to overall reading comprehension and academic achievement. Elementary teachers witness each day the struggle some of their students face as they labor through text that uses unfamiliar words. However, the enormous vocabulary demand on elementary students makes it impossible to provide direct instruction on each and every unfamiliar word they encounter. In order to do so, you would need to suspend any other teaching, and in the end it wouldn't be effective anyway because students wouldn't be getting the experiences they'd need to make word learning meaningful. Instead, students need a combination of approaches that together foster vocabulary acquisition and lead to more sophisticated language usage. The remainder of this book describes the components of an intentional approach for vocabulary development throughout subject areas. With this intentional approach, students become proficient readers, writers, and thinkers about the biological, physical, artistic, social, and literary world around them. In other words, the focus on subject area vocabulary ensures their entrance into the wide world of knowledge.

Make It Intentional

A Framework for Daily Word Learning

PROBABLY THE MOST IMPORTANT, YET RARELY ADDRESSED, aspect of an intentional vocabulary initiative is word selection. But we confess that we weren't always very good at this. Doug remembers opening the required textbook and preteaching, as it was called at that point, the words identified in the passage. Not knowing whether or not his students already understood the words, Doug followed the advice in the textbook and told a group of kindergartners all about caterpillars before reading the selection, *The Very Hungry Caterpillar* (Carle 1970). For Doug, all vocabulary was based on the readings students were doing.

Nancy remembers her first year of teaching. She was given a list of words that her third graders had to know. She divided the list into equal groups such that students had to learn seven to ten words per week. One of the weeks included the words *rabbit, cotton, gallon, lettuce, wedding, saddle, ferry,* and *equally*. As you can see, these words all have medial double consonants. The words Nancy taught were never connected to things students were reading, but they were organized in ways that should have helped students remember parts or conditions of the words.

Thankfully, both of us required our students to read a lot. Wide reading probably saved them from some of the less effective teaching practices we used. Fellow teachers often tell us they wish they could have their first year of teaching back to do it all again! And we'll come back to this aspect—extending subject matter vocabulary knowledge through wide reading—in Chapter 6 of this book. But we have to ask ourselves how much better our students might have achieved had they experienced a combination of wide reading *and* intentional vocabulary instruction. Of course, this begs a whole new set of questions. Which words? What is the best way to teach the selected words? How do students become independent vocabulary learners? As Beck, McKeown, and Kucan (2002) remind us, we don't teach words just because they are *in* context; we teach words because students can learn *from* contexts.

Before we consider approaches to subject area vocabulary instruction, we have to decide which words we should teach. As you might imagine, selecting words to teach has been a controversial matter.

■ Selecting Words to Teach

Probably the most important question you'll be asked relative to vocabulary instruction is "Which words will you teach?" Once upon a time, our answer to this question was to focus on the words that students would encounter in their reading. This answer is faulty for a number of reasons, not the least of which is that this approach limits the range of words to those currently appearing in the books students are reading. Please don't misunderstand what we are saying—selecting vocabulary from a reading is useful and necessary. However, this approach to vocabulary selection, *when used in isolation*, is insufficient because it leaves too much to chance. Students need intentional

Independent reading

Students need intentional instruction on a wider range of content words at their grade level than the text can possibly offer up, and it creates the false impression that reading the text is the best and chief forum for learning new words. Research shows that some words can be learned from reading, but not until students encounter the new words repeatedly—through reading many other texts, engaging in verbal discussion, and so on.

A sole focus on text-based word selection also doesn't capitalize on all the books that students might want to read independently. Consider Michael, a fourth grader, who wants to work one day for the San Diego Zoo. If he were taught only words from the books he's currently reading in school, it's unlikely that he would spend much time in the world of words that interest him. Fortunately, his teacher knows Michael's goal and encourages him to learn words related to the biological world. The school librarian gave him a copy of *The Snake Scientist* (Montgomery 1999), a book filled with pictures and information about snakes and the people who study them. She also introduced him to a collection of videos on exotic animal care. In doing so, she introduced Michael to a host of words that weren't found in his current readings but would be useful as he organized his thinking about animals and their care. Intentional vocabulary instruction involves keeping apace of our students' interests and improvising easy, authentic word learning to support their pursuits.

Narrowing the Possibilities by Sorting Words into Categories

Today, we're much more thoughtful when answering the questions we're asked about word selection. We think about the type of words that students need to know. As you no doubt recall from Chapter 1, words are often instructionally divided into three categories:

Tier 1, or General, Words: Commonplace words that students typically learn from interacting with other people or from their reading.

Tier 2, or Specialized, Words: Words that change their meaning based on the discipline in which they are used. These words are high frequency, meaning students will encounter them often in their reading. When students encounter a meaning of the word they aren't familiar with, they can get confused. Typically, students can define these words with easier words.

Tier 3, or Technical, Words: Words that are specific to a content area or discipline. These words occur infrequently but can be barriers to understanding content. Students typically do not know these words and have a hard time defining and using them.

Let's Try It: Analyzing a Typical Textbook Passage

Let's consider a typical text passage and identify the Tier 1, Tier 2, and Tier 3 words. This passage comes from a book commonly used to teach students about George Washington and the Revolutionary War. The opening three paragraphs read:

> On an October day in 1753, Robert Dinwiddie, Royal Governor of His Majesty's Colony in Virginia, sat in his office in Williamsburg, the capital of Virginia, reading the latest reports from the frontier. The French were causing trouble again, pushing their way into British land. There was a whiff of war in the air.
>
> Dinwiddie must have realized that Virginia's western boundary was fuzzy. Some Virginians even said that their colony stretched across the continent. But Dinwiddie knew that grand old claim was not realistic. He needed only turn to a map to see North America as it really was.
>
> Thirteen British Colonies stretched along the Atlantic Coast from New Hampshire to Georgia, with a long piece of Massachusetts land

called Maine in the north and, south of Georgia, a small piece of land called British Florida. Spain held the rest of Florida, along with most of the land west of the Mississippi River. The French occupied land in the Mississippi Valley called Louisiana and much of the land north of the Saint Lawrence River. They called that possession New France. If the French kept expanding their hold, they could link their southern lands with New France. (Allen 2004, 1–2)

Of course there is no scientific way to identify specifically which words would be placed into the various categories. Typically, we put words in the general category if they are common enough that most of our students know them. We put words in the specialized category if our students can generally define them with terms that are less specific or if the words have multiple meanings and the meaning might interfere with understanding. And finally, we put words in the technical category when they are specifically aligned with the content under investigation. While this may differ slightly from the organizational system developed by Beck and her colleagues (2002), it has worked for us in our efforts to focus on vocabulary. Using these lenses, we selected words from the George Washington

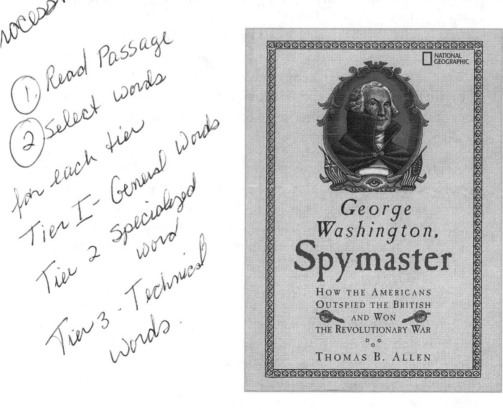

Process:
1. Read Passage
2. Select words for each tier
Tier 1 - General Words
Tier 2 Specialized word
Tier 3 - Technical Words.

General (Tier 1)	Specialized (Tier 2)	Technical (Tier 3)
whiff	office	Royal
war	capital	Governor
fuzzy	reports	Majesty
grand	frontier	Colony
realistic	western	continent
	boundary	
	claim	
	held/hold	
	occupied	
	possession	

Figure 2.1 *Selected words from* George Washington, Spymaster *(Allen 2004)*

passage and identified which tier they were in. Our analysis can be found in Figure 2.1.

As you can see, we did not include the proper nouns, such as the names of people, states, and countries. We assumed that students would have experience with these words based on the fact that they were learning about American history. We'd also provide context for this passage by having students first look at a map so they would have a visual image of the locations being discussed as they read the passage.

The Semi-finalists: Words That Might Be Worth Teaching

So which words would we focus on? Words that *might* need instructional attention. This simple analysis revealed fifteen words in the specialized or technical category that are candidates for intentional instruction. That doesn't mean that these fifteen words should necessarily all be taught. We know that there is a limit to the number of individual words a student can learn in any given week. Given this, you want to narrow down the number of words. We know that this isn't an easy process, but we have identified a number of questions that we can ask ourselves as we determine which words receive instructional attention and which do not. We have developed these questions after analyzing the recommendations of a number of vocabulary scholars, including Graves (2006), Nagy (1988), and Marzano and Pickering (2005). Figure 2.2 contains the topics we consider in selecting words as well as the questions we ask ourselves.

Topic	Questions to Ask
Representation	• Is the word representative of a family of words that students should know? • Is the concept represented by the word critical to understanding the text? • Is the word a label for an idea that students need to know? • Does the word represent an idea that is essential for understanding another concept?
Repeatability	• Is the word used again in this text? If so, does the word occur often enough to be redundant? • Will the word be used again during the school year?
Transportability	• Will the word be used in group discussions? • Will the word be used in writing tasks? • Will the word be used in other content or subject areas?
Contextual Analysis	• Can students use context clues to determine the correct or intended meaning of the word without instruction?
Structural Analysis	• Can students use structural analysis to determine the correct or intended meaning of the word without instruction?
Cognitive Load	• Have I identified too many words for students to successfully integrate?

Figure 2.2 *Considerations for selecting vocabulary words*

The Finalists and Why We Chose Them

Based on the questions in Figure 2.2, we selected six words from the George Washington text to teach. From Tier 2, we selected *held/hold*, *occupied*, and *possession*. We did so because these words are conceptually related and we know that this helps students transfer words into their knowledge base. In addition, these words are being used in very specific ways (related to social studies) that are not the ways in which they are commonly used. From Tier 3, we chose *Colony* and *continent*. These two words are essential to understanding early U.S. history. We believe that students will learn the roles of leaders (*Governor*, *His Majesty*) and about royalty in units of study that focus more specifically on these topics.

Of course, there is no one right answer to the specific words that you could choose to teach from this reading selection. The choice depends, in part, on the point of the school year in which the reading occurs, the assessed needs of students, and the range of instructional materials students will come in contact with.

Key in Selection

That said, we can generalize that systematic vocabulary instruction requires that teachers

1. know that *they* have to choose words—it's not a decision that should be left to textbook writers;

2. know from where to choose words; and   *separate out*

3. know how to categorize words in order to then winnow the possibilities of what to teach. This requires a decision-making model for selecting those big-bang-for-your-buck words that crack open key content understandings and that moonlight, so to speak, by helping kids infer meanings of many other words via common roots, prefixes, or suffixes. Words such as *judge*, *judgment*, *judicial*, and *prejudice* are some examples of these words.

A Decision-Making Model to Further Guide Your Word Selection

The work of Nagy (1988), Marzano and Pickering (2005), and Graves (2006) has informed our understanding of how to select words. To help you select your heavy hitters, it's helpful to evaluate the words you're considering from these vantage points:

How to select the words: Consider

- Is the word representative?

- Is it repeatable?

- Is it transportable?

- Is it best understood by students through contextual analysis?

- Is it best understood by students through structural analysis?

- Does it overburden the cognitive load?

① **REPRESENTATION**   Representation may be the aspect most frequently used by teachers when choosing a word for vocabulary instruction. Is the term representative of an important idea or concept? These words often come in the form of labels, such as *energy*, *patriot*, and *parallelogram*. At other times, it may be a gateway word for a series of related words. For instance, teaching *create* can lead to learning a number of variants, including *creator*, *creative*, and *recreation*.

REPEATABILITY   If a word is going to be used repeatedly, either within a unit of instruction or throughout the school year, it may be a good candidate for intentional instruction. Novel words that appear only once are not good choices because the learner won't receive multiple exposures to the word—a necessary condition of vocabulary learning (Stahl and Fairbanks 1986).

TRANSPORTABILITY   A third consideration in selecting a word for instruction is transportability. Is it likely that this word will be useful in another learning arrangement, such as a classroom discussion or written assignment? Words that are transportable may be useful in other content areas as well, such as the word *temperate*, which is used in English to describe an even-mannered character and in science to describe a mild climate.

CONTEXTUAL ANALYSIS   Contextual analysis requires looking at the context in which a word is used rather than viewing the word in isolation. If a term used in a reading is accompanied by surrounding words or phrases that define the word, then it is probably not necessary to provide direct instruction for this word.

STRUCTURAL ANALYSIS   As with context, the structure of the word may be sufficient for your students to infer the meaning. This judgment requires that you know your students well and are familiar with their exposure to the prefix, root, and suffix in the word. For example, a fifth-grade teacher might decide not to explicitly teach *information* because the affixes and root present in this term are apparent.

COGNITIVE LOAD   Unlike the other elements, consideration of cognitive load has less to do with the word itself and more to do with the learning context. At some point, the sheer number of words is daunting, and vocabulary instruction can detract from learning content—a bit like the tail wagging the dog. There aren't any hard-and-fast rules about what constitutes the right cognitive load, as it varies by learner and content. Our very informal rule of thumb has been to try to limit ourselves to two to three words per lesson, knowing that at some point students can't assimilate any more information.

Much in the spirit of that famous movie line "Show me the money," we imagine at this point you're saying to yourself, *Man, enough already, just give me the word lists!* You may even have flipped to the index, looking for a list or two. The temptation to dive into a word list is strong. Word lists convey a sense of completeness, especially when they are categorized by grade or content level. We find lists to be very useful, too, but only when balanced against an understanding of the types of words as well as a method for deselecting ones that are not needed. In other words, we use lists to inform our instruction, not formulate it. Keeping in mind the last few pages of discussion on types of words and a method for selecting words for systematic instruction will take you further in your teaching than any list, so thanks for hanging in there.

Using Word Lists to Inform Instruction

Who doesn't love a list? Getting to the end of one is a satisfying experience, be it a grocery, chore, or holiday gift list. David Letterman makes a top ten list every night he broadcasts. The same holds true for vocabulary word lists. Many of us may be familiar with commonly used lists, such as the Dolch sight word list. This list of 220 words has been around for many decades and has been utilized in nearly every K–3 classroom in the country. But there are other lists that are helpful in developing an intentional vocabulary initiative. Let's examine three types of word lists: general academic terms, basic English words, and word-part lists.

Academic Word Lists

Academic word lists are useful because they highlight terms commonly used in different content areas, such as science, social studies, mathematics, and the arts. These are composed mostly of Tier 1 (general vocabulary) and Tier 2 (specialized and multiple-meaning words).

One of our favorites comes from the work of Avril Coxhead of Massey University in New Zealand. She analyzed the running text of 414 textbooks from the major content areas and identified the most frequently used terms. She eliminated the first 2,000, as they consisted of sight words and other simple terms. She then applied further criteria regarding the range of texts in which terms appeared as well as their frequency, and she clustered them by word families (Coxhead 2000). The resulting 570 most frequently used word families include words such as *data*, *procedure*, *response*, and *theory* and can be found at http://language.massey.ac.nz/staff/awl/awlinfo.shtml.

The Academic Word List can be sorted in a number of different ways, depending on the purpose. Not every word on the list is suitable for instruction at the elementary level, but it is an excellent starting point for choosing targeted terms, especially from the early lists. Colleagues at our school have used the list to identify terms used on tests and have incorporated these to strengthen students' test-wise strategies. Upper grade-level teams have worked together to locate terminology from the list used frequently in their own classes. In addition, because the words are arranged according to word families, teachers are able to extend student knowledge to related words.

Ogden's Basic English Word List

Many of our students are new to English and are simultaneously challenged to learn English and learn *in* English (Fisher, Rothenberg, and Frey 2007). These learners need to acquire a tremendous volume of vocabulary in a short period of time. We were intrigued when we learned of a list developed in 1930 by Charles K. Ogden. His list began as a constructed language of 850 words that are phonetically regular and therefore easy to pronounce (see Figure 2.3). In addition, these words can be used in combination with others to form other words. For a time after World War II, it was even touted as a universal language that could bring about world peace. While we haven't had quite that much success with it, Ogden's list has been a great tool for working with English learners who are new to the language. Ogden's list has acquired a new life in the twenty-first century, as it forms the core of the 2,000-word list used to write entries for the Simple English Wikipedia (http://simple.wikipedia.org).

Word-Part Lists

Vocabulary instruction should always look toward the ultimate goal, which is student independence, since it's a certainty that you won't be there every time students encounter an unfamiliar word. Students' ability to structurally analyze a word to identify its word parts and then make an educated prediction about the meaning will serve them well. You use this skill all the time. For example, Doug has been studying about the brain and has encountered quite a volume of unfamiliar vocabulary. When he read the phrase *sagittal plane* (a term used to describe a view of the brain that goes through the center from front to back), he was initially confused. Where did that word come from? However, he quickly made a connection between the diagram and the word *Sagittarius*, the archer in astrology. He visualized an archer with his bow drawn back and then understood the derivation of the word.

While it may not seem that elementary students can learn Latin and Greek words, there are several pathways that can ignite their learning. Consider, for example, the ability of even young children to name dinosaurs. *Triceratops* ("three-horned face") and *Tyrannosaurus rex* ("tyrant lizard king") consist of Latin words that vividly describe these creatures. Roman and Greek mythologies illustrate their characters' names, as in the tale of Juventas ("youth"), a Roman goddess who collected a coin from

Operations (100 words)
come, get, give, go, keep, let, make, put, seem, take, be, do, have, say, see, send, may, will, about, across, after, against, among, at, before, between, by, down, from, in, off, on, over, through, to, under, up, with, as, for, of, till, than, a, the, all, any, every, little, much, no, other, some, such, that, this, I, he, you, who, and, because, but, or, if, though, while, how, when, where, why, again, ever, far, forward, here, near, now, out, still, then, there, together, well, almost, enough, even, not, only, quite, so, very, tomorrow, yesterday, north, south, east, west, please, yes

Things (400 general words)
account, act, addition, adjustment, advertisement, agreement, air, amount, amusement, animal, answer, apparatus, approval, argument, art, attack, attempt, attention, attraction, authority, back, balance, base, behavior, belief, birth, bit, bite, blood, blow, body, brass, bread, breath, brother, building, burn, burst, business, butter, canvas, care, cause, chalk, chance, change, cloth, coal, color, comfort, committee, company, comparison, competition, condition, connection, control, cook, copper, copy, cork, cotton, cough, country, cover, crack, credit, crime, crush, cry, current, curve, damage, danger, daughter, day, death, debt, decision, degree, design, desire, destruction, detail, development, digestion, direction, discovery, discussion, disease, disgust, distance, distribution, division, doubt, drink, driving, dust, earth, edge, education, effect, end, error, event, example, exchange, existence, expansion, experience, expert, fact, fall, family, father, fear, feeling, fiction, field, fight, fire, flame, flight, flower, fold, food, force, form, friend, front, fruit, glass, gold, government, grain, grass, grip, group, growth, guide, harbor, harmony, hate, hearing, heat, help, history, hole, hope, hour, humor, ice, idea, impulse, increase, industry, ink, insect, instrument, insurance, interest, invention, iron, jelly, join, journey, judge, jump, kick, kiss, knowledge, land, language, laugh, law, lead, learning, leather, letter, level, lift, light, limit, linen, liquid, list, look, loss, love, machine, man, manager, mark, market, mass, meal, measure, meat, meeting, memory, metal, middle, milk, mind, mine, minute, mist, money, month, morning, mother, motion, mountain, move, music, name, nation, need, news, night, noise, note, number, observation, offer, oil, operation, opinion, order, organization, ornament, owner, page, pain, paint, paper, part, paste, payment, peace, person, place, plant, play, pleasure, point, poison, polish, porter, position, powder, power, price, print, process, produce, profit, property, prose, protest, pull, punishment, purpose, push, quality, question, rain, range, rate, ray, reaction, reading, reason, record, regret, relation, religion, representative, request, respect, rest, reward, rhythm, rice, river, road, roll, room, rub, rule, run, salt, sand, scale, science, sea, seat, secretary, selection, self, sense, servant, sex, shade, shake, shame, shock, side, sign, silk, silver, sister, size, sky, sleep, slip, slope, smash, smell, smile, smoke, sneeze, snow, soap, society, son, song, sort, sound, soup, space, stage, start, statement, steam, steel, step, stitch, stone, stop, story, stretch, structure, substance, sugar, suggestion, summer, support, surprise, swim, system, talk, taste, tax, teaching, tendency, test, theory, thing, thought, thunder, time, tin, top, touch, trade, transport, trick, trouble, turn, twist, unit, use, value, verse, vessel, view, voice, walk, war, wash, waste, water, wave, wax, way, weather, week, weight, wind, wine, winter, woman, wood, wool, word, work, wound, writing, year

Things (200 picturable words)
angle, ant, apple, arch, arm, army, baby, bag, ball, band, basin, basket, bath, bed, bee, bell, berry, bird, blade, board, boat, bone, book, boot, bottle, box, boy, brain, brake, branch, brick, bridge, brush, bucket, bulb, button, cake, camera, card, cart, carriage, cat, chain, cheese, chest, chin, church, circle, clock, cloud, coat, collar, comb, cord, cow, cup, curtain, cushion, dog, door, drain, drawer, dress, drop, ear, egg, engine, eye, face, farm, feather, finger, fish, flag, floor, fly, foot, fork, fowl, frame, garden, girl, glove, goat, gun, hair, hammer, hand, hat, head, heart, hook, horn, horse, hospital, house, island, jewel, kettle, key, knee, knife, knot, leaf, leg, library, line, lip, lock, map, match, monkey, moon, mouth, muscle, nail, neck, needle, nerve, net, nose, nut, office, orange, oven, parcel, pen, pencil, picture, pig, pin, pipe, plane, plate, plough/plow, pocket, pot, potato, prison, pump, rail, rat, receipt, ring, rod, roof, root, sail, school, scissors, screw, seed, sheep, shelf, ship, shirt, shoe, skin, skirt, snake, sock, spade, sponge, spoon, spring, square, stamp, star, station, stem, stick, stocking, stomach, store, street, sun, table, tail, thread, throat, thumb, ticket, toe, tongue, tooth, town, train, tray, tree, trousers, umbrella, wall, watch, wheel, whip, whistle, window, wing, wire, worm

Qualities (100 general words)
able, acid, angry, automatic, beautiful, black, boiling, bright, broken, brown, cheap, chemical, chief, clean, clear, common, complex, conscious, cut, deep, dependent, early, elastic, electric, equal, fat, fertile, first, fixed, flat, free, frequent, full, general, good, great, grey/gray, hanging, happy, hard, healthy, high, hollow, important, kind, like, living, long, male, married, material, medical, military, natural, necessary, new, normal, open, parallel, past, physical, political, poor, possible, present, private, probable, quick, quiet, ready, red, regular, responsible, right, round, same, second, separate, serious, sharp, smooth, sticky, stiff, straight, strong, sudden, sweet, tall, thick, tight, tired, true, violent, waiting, warm, wet, wide, wise, yellow, young

Qualities (50 opposites)
awake, bad, bent, bitter, blue, certain, cold, complete, cruel, dark, dead, dear, delicate, different, dirty, dry, false, feeble, female, foolish, future, green, ill, last, late, left, loose, loud, low, mixed, narrow, old, opposite, public, rough, sad, safe, secret, short, shut, simple, slow, small, soft, solid, special, strange, thin, white, wrong

Source: Ogden, C. K. No date. "Ogden's Basic English Word List—in His Order." http://ogden.basic-english.org/words.html

Figure 2.3 *Ogden's Basic Word List*

boys who wore a toga for the first time. Attention to words like these serves as a gateway to other terms. *Triceratops* leads to *tricycle*; *Tyrannosaurus* is a short step to *tyrant*; *Juventas* leads to *juvenile*. There are many websites featuring Latin and Greek roots, and most have been developed for elementary and secondary students. One of our favorites is sponsored by the Kent (Washington) School District and can be found at www.kent.k12.wa.us/ksd/MA/resources/greek_and_latin_roots/transition.html. In addition, there are good print-based materials for elementary teachers, especially *Words Their Way* (Bear et al. 2008) and *The Vocabulary Teacher's Book of Lists* (Fry 2004).

In addition to learning the derivational meanings of Latin and Greek root words, students benefit from understanding prefixes and suffixes (collectively called *affixes*). Teaching students the high-frequency affixes can equip them with the tools they need to deconstruct an unfamiliar word in order to understand it. For example, the prefix *un-* appears in 26 percent of all English words with a prefix, while the suffix variant *-s* or *-es* is featured in 31 percent of all suffixed words (White, Sowell, and Yanagihara 1989). A chart of the most common affixes appears in Figure 2.4.

So far, we have discussed the types of vocabulary, a decision-making model for identifying words for possible intentional instruction, and examples of useful word lists. The final step in selecting words is identifying words as a grade-level team. This helps ensure that students move through a sequence of classes with a growing base of vocabulary knowledge.

Selecting Technical Words for a Grade Level

In many schools, teachers who teach the same grade level are identifying technical vocabulary that requires instruction. Teachers meet in grade-level teams to identify essential terms and all agree to teach them during each unit of instruction. This approach is consistent with the curricular initiatives common to school reform, especially standards alignment and the development of pacing guides (e.g., Wiggins and McTighe 2005). By agreeing to teach specific technical words, teachers ensure that students arrive in subsequent grades with grounding in the targeted terminology. For example, it is useful for the fourth-grade teachers to know that the third-grade teachers taught students Tier 2 words such as *star*, *pattern*, and *distant* as well as Tier 3 words like *evaporation*, *lunar cycle*, and *planet* during a unit on earth science.

Two sources of information are useful for identifying grade-level vocabulary. The first is the state content standards document, whose descriptions feature a large number of vocabulary terms. We often think of these documents as being written for an adult audience, but they can be a treasure

Rank	Prefix	Percent of All Prefixed Words	Suffix	Percent of All Suffixed Words
1	un-	26	-s, -es	31
2	re-	14	-ed	20
3	in-, im-, il-, ir- (not)	11	-ing	14
4	dis-	7	-ly	7
5	en-, em-	4	-er, -or (agent)	4
6	non-	4	-ion, -tion, -ation, -ition	4
7	in-, im- (in)	3	-able, -ible	2
8	over-	3	-al, -ial	1
9	mis-	3	-y	1
10	sub-	3	-ness	1
11	pre-	3	-ity, -ty	1
12	inter-	3	-ment	1
13	fore-	3	-ic	1
14	de-	2	-ous, -eous, -ious	1
15	trans-	2	-en	1
16	super-	1	-er (comparative)	1
17	semi-	1	-ive, -ative, -tive	1
18	anti-	1	-ful	1
19	mid-	1	-less	1
20	under- (too little)	1	-est	1
	all others	3	all others	1

Source: White, T. G., Sowell, J., and Yanagihara, A. (1989, January). Teaching Elementary Students to Use Word-Part Clues. *The Reading Teacher,* 42 (4), 302–308. Reprinted with permission of the International Reading Association.

Figure 2.4 *The twenty most frequent affixes in printed school English*

trove of student vocabulary. For example, the second-grade science standards document for California contains the following technical vocabulary terms: *organisms, offspring, parents,* and *butterflies.* In addition, these specialized terms appear in the same standard: *predictable, cycles, stages, environment, population,* and *variation* (California Department of Education 2000). (Interestingly, several of these Tier 2 words appear on the Academic Word List as well.)

A second source for identifying vocabulary words is the curricular materials themselves. The glossary and bolded words in the textbook are obvious choices for consideration, and most instructor materials also contain additional support materials for vocabulary instruction. It should be noted that we are discussing vocabulary lists from textbooks last. While they are a good source, they are not going to be very useful if merely photocopied and assigned to students to learn somehow. Effective vocabulary development requires careful and purposeful selection of words. It also requires that the instruction of vocabulary honors what we know about good teaching and learning.

■ Intentional Instruction of the Words You Select

Since this entire book is about how to develop subject area vocabulary knowledge, we'll resist the urge to tell you everything now. Instead, we will describe an instructional framework useful in fostering word knowledge. This model doesn't depend on hours of instruction devoted to learning just a few words, but rather requires that vocabulary development become a natural part of classroom instruction. In other words, intentional instruction of vocabulary doesn't stand apart from the content—it is a necessary factor in content mastery.

Our framework for intentional vocabulary instruction is based on a gradual release of responsibility model (e.g., Pearson and Gallagher 1983). In essence, the gradual release of responsibility model suggests that teachers move from assuming all of the responsibility to sharing responsibility with students to transferring responsibility to students. This release of responsibility occurs at the macro and micro levels as teachers plan daily lessons, units of study, and entire semesters and school years. In our work on vocabulary, we have found three components of the gradual release of responsibility especially helpful: *demonstrations*, *practice with peers*, and *independent applications*. In addition, our work with entire school buildings suggests that a schoolwide focus on vocabulary can raise the level of word consciousness and create a much needed focus on word learning.

Demonstrations: The Importance of Teacher Modeling

One component of the gradual release of responsibility requires that teachers demonstrate and model their own thinking and understanding. Teacher read-alouds, think-alouds, and shared readings are particularly effective ways for providing the modeling that students need. These approaches can be used to raise word consciousness, teach word-solving strategies, and foster vocabulary metacognition. They can also be used to demonstrate the importance of vocabulary in understanding texts. For example, consider the following passage from the book *Lives of the Presidents* (Krull 1998) that we read to a group of fifth-grade students:

Thomas Jefferson matured into an unusually well-read lawyer—and our most versatile president. Everything interested him, from traveling by balloon to playing violin (which he did for as much as three hours per day), from gardening to nature (his idea of a great time was tasting fresh asparagus, smelling the lilacs in bloom, and seeing the first whippoorwill of the season) to architecture (he designed one of the most beautiful homes in America—Monticello, his palatial mountaintop estate).

He wanted to include his wife, Martha Wayles Skelton, known as Patty, in all he did. But seven pregnancies in ten years weakened her, and her death at age thirty-three devastated him. Immersing himself in politics was his way of getting over the loss, as was lavishing attention on his two surviving daughters (and later his eleven grandchildren, thanks to whom Jefferson has more living descendants than any other president). (19)

There's quite a bit of content knowledge packed in those few sentences. When Nancy read this to her students, she stated, "As I read that, I noticed the way that the author created the scene with words. In the first paragraph, we learn that Mr. Jefferson had a lot of interests and knew a lot about the world. I like that she says Jefferson was *versatile* and then describes all of the different things he could do. I remember that *versa-* means to turn, like when I say *reverse*. So *versatile* is a good word for telling us how he was always turning to some new interest.

"In the second paragraph, we learn more about Jefferson's choice to go into politics, which we know means government and elected officials. I remember that Jefferson was *versatile* and probably could have done anything he wanted to, but she says that he *immersed* himself in politics to get over all of the deaths in his family—not only his wife, but also five children. I'm not sure why he chose politics over the other things he was interested in, but I bet the author will tell us as we read on. I was also interested to learn that Jefferson has more *descendants*—which is the opposite of *ancestors*, remember—than any other president."

Nancy showed her students how she grouped words conceptually, analyzed those words to reach a conclusion, and extended her thinking to model how an expert understands content material. She didn't need to hang up a banner that said, "Vocabulary Time." Instead, she incorporated vocabulary development seamlessly into her content teaching.

Peer Practice: The Importance of Consolidating New Learning

Building word learning through peer interaction is another component of our instructional design. We know it is not enough for teachers to model the use of vocabulary; students must have lots of opportunities to build their nascent knowledge using oral language. You can't be the arbiter of all that talk, so you'll need to structure lots of opportunities for students to work in peer groups. We know you're thinking that a social event seems to break out each time you allow some peer talk in your classroom. We assure you that the strategies we discuss in Chapter 4 will at least result in talk that is on topic.

Oral language experiences are essential to the social and cognitive development of young learners. These opportunities are even more critical for young children who are simultaneously learning English and learning in English (Pollard-Durodola, Mathes, and Vaughn 2006). The intent of these interactions is to provide learners with a chance to clarify their understanding of new words, apply these words to new situations, and deepen their conceptual understanding by linking prior knowledge to new learning.

We know that students build their understanding of subject matter word learning through activities that cause them to discuss, clarify, and collaborate. Our experiences suggest that having students produce something as a result of their collaborative efforts results in increased use of targeted vocabulary. The use of words with peers provides an opportunity for consolidation of learning. Accordingly, we regularly use semantic feature analyses and word maps. We also ask students to work together to develop concept circles, collaborative posters, and shades-of-meaning cards. We invite them to make predictions about readings using text impressions and to think aloud with one another as they engage in partner reading. The discussions that emerge from these interactions foster a deepening understanding of vocabulary and the related concepts under investigation. We discuss these instructional routines in more detail in Chapters 3, 4, and 5.

Consider the conversation a group of fifth graders where having about the human body. At the point that this conversation occurred, they had experienced a number of teacher read-alouds, watched a short film about the body, and measured their bodies and labeled various parts. The task for this particular day was to create a collaborative poster about one of the body systems. One group worked on the respiratory system while another group worked on the digestive system, and still another worked on the nervous system. Listening in as the group focused on the nervous system completed their task clearly demonstrates their use and understanding of subject area vocabulary. They had a number of books at their station, including *Think, Think, Think: Learning About Your Brain* (Nettleton 2004) and *The Brain: Our Nervous System* (Simon 1997).

James: But I don't get it. How do you know which is which?

Maria: I remember it this way: The sensory nerve brings information to your brain.

Kevin: Yeah, and the motor nerve travels away from your brain to make you move.

James: So when I touch something, like this pencil, the sensory nerve is sending information to my brain.

Maria: Yes, but you have lots of sensory nerves. Look at this picture again [*points to a graphic in a book*]. The hot pan sends a message from the sensory nerves to the brain. See this area called "sensory area"? That's where the brain figures out what the information is. Then, see how it sends another message to move the hand? The motor neurons send that message to the muscles.

Kevin: You gotta think of them as one-way streets. The information only goes one way. Sensory to the brain; motor away from the brain. Motor equals muscles, get it?

Maria: Exactly!

The conversation these students had demonstrates their collective ability to integrate vocabulary, both specialized and technical, into their thinking. In using and discussing these terms, students built their understanding of both the content and the words used to discuss the content. If students are not provided these opportunities to negotiate with their peers, learning becomes a passive activity in which words are held in the air of the classroom, but not the minds of the learners.

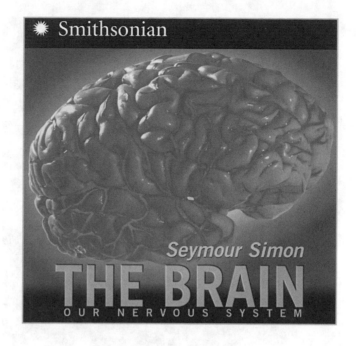

Independent Activities: The Importance of Application

At some point, students need time to apply what they have learned through teacher modeling and peer collaboration by consolidating their understanding of the vocabulary. We want individuals to utilize writing in order to strengthen their own command of the language. As we explain in Chapter 5, activities such as word sorts and A–Z charts encourage students to group and categorize concepts. Students also used words in generative sentences, journal writing, and paragraph frames. In addition, they need to further develop their metacognitive awareness about how they learn words, so they assess their knowledge using vocabulary self-awareness techniques and develop Frayer model vocabulary cards (e.g., Frayer, Frederick, and Klausmeier 1969, and discussed in Chapter 5) when they need more formal study techniques.

Once again, these individual activities can be integrated into the content instruction of the classroom. For example, word learning during mathematics is embedded into journal writing when the teacher invites his students to use *base*, *bisect*, and *volume* to explain how a problem is solved. It is at this stage, through individual activities, that teachers should assess students' vocabulary knowledge. Simple assessments requiring students to use words can provide teachers with information about which students have mastered the vocabulary and which students require additional instruction.

Writing and reading are daily occurrences

As we've said before, the most successful vocabulary instruction is embedded within the overall instructional design of the class. However, attention to vocabulary development within this framework can increase word learning. In Figure 2.5, you will find a five-day schedule of the fifth-grade human body unit discussed earlier. Notice all the opportunities these students had to acquire and use targeted vocabulary during this unit of instruction.

Word Consciousness: The Importance of a Schoolwide Focus

Vocabulary demand far exceeds the capacity of any teacher or school to directly teach each word, and yet many students seem to acquire a rich vocabulary that outstrips the amount formally presented. These learners are able to accomplish this through extensive reading. The incidental vocabulary learning that takes place when a reader is engaged with a text that is not too difficult can range from anywhere between five and fifteen new words out of every one hundred unknown ones (Nagy and Herman 1987).

	Monday	Tuesday	Wednesday	Thursday	Friday
Demonstrations	Educational film on the human body Introduction of terms	Teacher read-aloud: focus on word solving Teacher modeling on using word wall in writing	Teacher read-aloud: focus on using resources	Teacher read-aloud: focus on contextual clues	Teacher modeling of writing using targeted vocabulary
Practice with Peers	Partner discussion using terms	Measure bodies and label parts	Reciprocal teaching with textbook passage	Complete a semantic feature analysis of concepts	Collaborative poster Groups develop concept circles for classmates on their body system
Independent Applications	Vocabulary self-awareness chart	Science journal writing using targeted vocabulary	Independent reading from class libary	Open word sort of terms	Science journal writing using targeted vocabulary

Figure 2.5 *Vocabulary instruction using a gradual release of responsibility approach*

Students need repeated exposures in authentic contexts to really understand a word. Wide reading provides this exposure as students read a variety of texts and genres. It's a numbers game, really—the more print material students come in contact with, the more exposure they have to familiar and unfamiliar vocabulary. Over time, they acquire new words and deepen their understanding of partially known ones.

Chapter 6 focuses on two well-known initiatives for increasing reading volume—sustained silent reading (SSR) and independent reading. SSR remains popular because of its effects on student motivation, interest, and academic achievement (Marzano 2004). It is typically designed as a fifteen- to twenty-minute daily period when students and teachers read materials of their own choosing, including nonacademic texts. This is often accomplished through a schoolwide initiative because it transmits the values of a school regarding reading and provides support for teachers who do not traditionally use a lot of reading material in the classroom.

Many teachers also incorporate independent reading of content-related texts in their classes. The amount of information derived from print increases as students get older, and they need time to process this information. (Most of us have learned by this time that telling them everything just doesn't work.) Independent reading sometimes includes textbook passages, but it is an ideal time to expose students to richly varied materials—after all, the textbook publishers are the first to tell you that no single textbook could contain all the information needed for any subject. Independent reading should provide students with opportunities to interact with main ideas under investigation as well as extensions of the topics.

■ The Takeaway

It isn't enough to merely present students with a list of words for them to memorize and regurgitate on the next quiz; words must be taught in a systematic and intentional way. This doesn't mean that content instruction must be pushed aside to make room for vocabulary, but it does mean that the two need to be consolidated so that word learning is a natural and necessary part of learning the content. The first step is to identify the general, specialized, and technical vocabulary necessary across a student's day. This is best done in grade-level collaborations with fellow instructors. An added benefit to this approach is that other educators are aware of what their students are learning. Some schools augment vocabulary development with a Words of the Week program that offers students additional exposure to words related through affixes and roots.

In order for word learning to be systematic and intentional, students need an instructional design that provides them with varied experience with words. This includes

- modeling by the teacher to raise word consciousness and show students problem-solving approaches to figuring out unfamiliar words;

- building subject area vocabulary knowledge through peer interactions;

- consolidating vocabulary knowledge through individual activities; and

- extending vocabulary and conceptual knowledge through wide reading.

In the following chapters we elaborate further on each of these components in the instructional design of subject area vocabulary development. Taken together, they help students learn words inside and out.

CHAPTER

3

Make It Transparent

Showing Students Your Thinking About Words

AMANDA ENTERED HER SIXTH-GRADE CLASSROOM after lunch and saw a few problems on the board. Some were unfamiliar to her; they had a number of operations in different parentheses. The first problem read: 6 + 4 × 7 − 3. Amanda's teacher, Ms. Tran, turned to her class, smiled, and joked, "It's all about the order, right? Just follow me and we'll make it out the other side." Mrs. Tran thought aloud as she solved each problem:

> Hmmm, the first thing I see is that the order in which the arithmetic is done may change the result. I have to pay close attention here. Multiplication and division are the first order of business for problem solving—they're more

important. I remember that I'm supposed to solve problems by moving left to right, stopping to taking care of any multiplication and division first.

So, 4 × 7 is 28. But then I keep reading the problem to see if there are any other places to multiply or divide. Nope, no more. So if I rewrite the problem with my new information, I get 6 + 28 − 3. The second time through, I look for opportunities to solve addition and subtraction, whichever comes first. So, 6 + 28 is 34, and then minus 3, which is 31. My answer is 31.

The second problem has added some parentheses. I remember that expressions within a pair of parentheses—those curved lines that surround numbers or words that look like rounded brackets—are to be computed *before* expressions outside the parentheses. I remember that without parentheses to show what calculation is to be done, multiplications and divisions are to be done before additions and subtractions. So the same numbers with added parentheses might change the answer. Let's try the second one: (6 + 4) × 7 − 3. So, with the parentheses rule, I know that I have to add 6 and 4 together first, which is 10. Then I go through looking for multiplication and division. And yes, I can multiply 10 × 7, which is 70, and then minus 3, which is 67. *Wow*, the same numbers with those added parentheses really changes the answer.

But look, there's a third one for me to do. It's got the same numbers, but with the parenthesis moved again: 6 + 4 × (7 − 3). I know that I have to solve inside the innermost parentheses first, and 7 minus 3 is 4. Then, I go through looking for multiplication and division, so I can't add the 6 and 4 together yet. Look, the 4 is multiplied by this 4, which is 16. Then I can add 6 to my 16 and get 22. Another different answer because of the parentheses!

In some classrooms, teachers tend to put a new kind of problem on the board and invite their students to do a swan dive into the deep end of the pool—that is, to do the problem independently—and then begin instruction after students struggle with it for a bit. Some teachers put a problem like these on the board and then ask students a series of questions about the problem, an approach that tends to make the advanced math students shine but undermine the confidence of other students. Instead, Mrs. Tran believes the most effective instructional move is to model her thinking using the vocabulary of a mathematician. For example, to start she said, "Multiplication and division have a higher priority in problem solving." Her modeling included the use of terms such as *expression*, *parentheses*, and *innermost*.

Amanda's teacher continued to model her thinking about these problems until they were solved. She then picked up the book she was reading aloud to the class, *A Gebra Named Al* (Isdell 1993), and began reading. In this part of the book, the characters are in a cave, which is symbolic of parentheses:

> Julie found herself in another small chamber, like the first they had entered. "What's this?" she demanded. "Aren't we supposed to be in a large cave?"
>
> "You always start from the innermost Parenthesis," Al reminded her.
>
> "Oh, right," Julie remembered. "You start at the innermost, do all the math there, and work outward. At least, that's what you were supposed to do with a math problem." (40)

Ms. Tran paused and shared her thinking. Again, she explained her understanding of order of operations and focused on the role that the parentheses play in determining the correct answer. Mrs. Tran often uses the first fifteen minutes of class in this manner, for she knows that students then go into the task with all her language and actions buzzing in their heads as they problem solve. A plethora of research supports Mrs. Tran's approach.

■ The Importance of Modeling

Humans have a profound ability to mimic what they see others say and do. This innate ability has served our species well for tens of thousands of years; it's how we learned to communicate and how we transmit information from one generation to the next. Through observations of others—our parents, for example—we acquire certain behaviors. As we observe others, we incorporate their models into our behavior. Who can forget the toddler who mimicked Mom's harried search for the car keys or talking to a friend on the phone? We remember an episode of *America's Funniest Home Videos* in which a young boy was "golfing" in his backyard. His mother asked, "Can you golf like Daddy?" Immediately, the child slammed the golf club to the ground and yelled "Damn it!" Yes, that's how Daddy plays golf.

Of course, most of the behaviors we incorporate into our patterns are more adaptive than our father's golfing performance. Just think back on all the things in your life you've watched another person do before you tried it on your own—skiing, playing tennis, using chopsticks for the first time. Most of us have vivid memories of learning to ride a bike or a parent patiently (or not!) teaching us how to drive a car. But learning to read? We might have a few flickering memories of pretend reading, phonics lessons in first grade, but then it's kind of a fast forward to full-tilt reading of *Charlotte's*

Web or *Charlie and the Chocolate Factory*! What happened in between? Alas, reading isn't a physical behavior. It's a cognitive one, a thinking task, and as such is invisible to others. As a result, we cannot directly demonstrate it. We have to talk about it. As Duffy noted, "The only way to model thinking is to talk about how to do it. That is, we provide a verbal description of the thinking one does or, more accurately, an *approximation* of the thinking involved (since there is no one way to do any reading task)" (2003, 11).

This is what Amanda's teacher did. She provided her students an approximation of the thinking required to solve problems using the correct order of operations. She did so by sharing her own thinking, explaining her thinking, and making an invisible process more transparent for her students. Importantly, Ms. Tran understands that this is not accomplished in a single teaching event; her use of modeling occurs many times a day, often using the same terms again and again. Over time, Amanda incorporated the thinking, procedures, and habits modeled by her teacher. On one afternoon, we heard Amanda say to a peer, "I can't just tell you the answer. Let me talk you through it. I can explain my thinking about this problem to you."

Let's look at two other teachers modeling their thinking. Paul Justice's third-grade students were studying native people and civilizations when he shared with them *Knots on a Counting Rope* (Martin and Archambault 1987). The words he read included these:

> I have already crossed some of the dark mountains.
>> There will be more, Boy.
>> Dark Mountains
>> are always around us.
>> They have no beginnings and . . .
>> . . . they have no endings.
> But we know they are there, Grandfather, when we suddenly feel afraid.
>> Yes, Boy . . . afraid to do
>> what we have to do.
> Will I always have to live in the dark?
>> Yes, Boy.
>> Your were born with a dark curtain
>> in front of your eyes.
> But there are many ways to see, Grandfather.

After reading the passage, Mr. Justice explained his thinking. He said, "There's been a lot of talk about dark mountains. The pictures make it look like it's dark outside. But on this page, Boy says, 'Will I always have to live in the dark?' Why would a person ask that if they could see? The sun will come up every morning and then there's light. Adding this question to the pictures and other parts of the story, I'm going to make a guess that he is blind. I don't know why else someone would ask that question, so that's my prediction for now.

"But as I think about this text, I think that there is another important message here. Grandfather says, 'Dark Mountains are always around us.' I don't think he means that there are dark mountains that are real. I think that he is using it as a symbol about danger and fear. I think that because people are usually afraid of things in the dark, and mountains are huge obstacles for people. So, I think he's created a symbol for us to understand that there will always be things that we are afraid of and that we have to conquer."

Similarly, kindergarten teacher Kelly Preston shared a piece of text with her students about advocacy called *Click, Clack, Moo: Cows That Type* (Cronin 2000). The first page reads:

> Farmer Brown has a problem.
> His cows like to type.
> All day long he hears
> Click, clack, **moo**.
> Click, clack, **moo**.
> Clickety, clack, **moo**.

Ms. Preston shared her thinking and understanding about this piece of text with her students and modeled her questioning. She said, "Cows that type? I wonder what they type all day. That's a good question for me to keep in my mind as I read. Now, if I were a cow, what would I want to type? Maybe I'd want to write my cow friends at other farms. Or maybe I'd want to write about my day, like a journal."

Several pages later in the book, the farmer receives a letter from the cows demanding electric blankets. Ms. Preston said, "Who would have guessed that the cows were cold? I guess they wanted to type a letter to ask for some electric blankets. I'm picturing that in my mind, cows with blankets on top of them. I can picture that. But I wonder where they will plug them in? I also wonder who will pay the electric bill for the cows? That could be a problem."

Of course, good teachers have always modeled to facilitate learning. Modeling has been used to improve student behavior (Wilford 2007), facili-

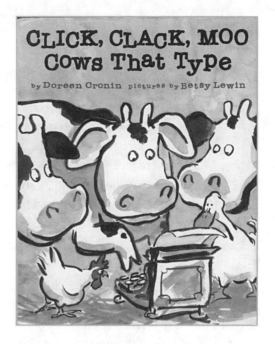

tate research writing for primary science students (Barclay and Traser 1999), and teach students how to have literature discussions (Recksiek 2005). Expert teachers know that modeling is a critical phase in developing student independence. Expert teachers also know that modeling alone is insufficient to change achievement (Fisher and Frey 2008). Students need opportunities to apply what they've seen modeled, to receive feedback on their attempts, and time to consolidate their understanding.

In this book, we give modeling bigger billing than it has received in other books on vocabulary, because our students do so much better when they've heard and watched us identify and solve unknown words and can then mimic our *procedures* for discerning meaning. We've got to get away from the mind-set that vocabulary instruction is about teaching specific words. Rather, it's about teaching specific strategies for approaching all words and remembering that the more we talk about and express an excitement and curiosity about new words, the more our students will absorb this attitude and bring it to bear in their own reading and writing (Blachowicz and Fisher 2005). And finally, we need to model when and how to consult resources when our word-solving strategies fall short.

Interestingly, there is some concern about modeling as a component of vocabulary instruction. For example, Beck, McKeown, and Kucan suggest that modeling "can be useful, but teachers should use it sparingly because it puts students in the passive role of overhearing the teacher thinking aloud" (2002, 41). They continue, suggesting that modeling be reserved for times in which students are being introduced to the idea of gaining meaning from context or when complicated or subtle context is being used. They suggest that students "be made part of the deriving-meaning process as soon as possible, queried along the way as meaning elements are derived from context" (41).

We understand this concern, and we are also concerned that some teachers may think they are modeling when they are merely explaining word meanings. We have also seen good modeling that simply went on for too long! When kept brief, five to ten minutes, as part of a systematic approach to vocabulary development, modeling is a powerful instructional component. Our classroom experience and research suggest that modeling, when used to establish word-solving procedures to determine meaning and not to teach specific words (e.g., Fisher, Frey, and Lapp 2008), is a powerful way of developing subject area vocabulary.

Our own recent research is anchored in a body of research on modeling and thinking aloud that suggests that modeling our thinking processes is a critical phase of instruction (e.g., Afflerbach and Johnston 1984; Bereiter and Bird 1985; Davey 1983; Wilhelm 2001). Simply asking students questions about words, especially in a whole-class format, is unlikely to ensure that all students learn to use new vocabulary. The one or two students participating in the back-and-forth dialogue with the teacher are probably learning, but what about the other twenty to thirty-five students in the class? Essentially, they fall into the passive role that Beck and her colleagues noted (2002).

Again, it is so tempting for content area teachers to teach specific words and keep moving forward, covering that curriculum. But in the end, this shortcut fails us because our students wind up dependent on us, and they flounder in the reading we assign because we haven't given them the mental models for solving unknown words *while engaged with texts*.

■ Modeling Procedures for Solving Words

We have organized teacher modeling of word-solving strategies into three components: context clues, morphology and word parts, and resources. In each of these cases, we'll look inside Amanda's classroom for examples.

Context Clues One of the ways that readers figure out unknown words is through the use of context clues. This is an example of an outside-of-the-word strategy. The goal of modeling context clues is to provide students with enough examples so that they can use this approach independently. Of course, context clues don't work 100 percent of the time, and students need examples of when this approach fails and what else they can do. Before we consider when to use context clues, let's note when they don't work.

In their study of basal reading programs, Beck, McKeown, and McCaslin (1983) identified four kinds of categories for natural contexts. Of these four categories, some are helpful and others are not. The continuum of contexts they identified spans from misdirective to nondirective to general to directive. *Misdirective* contexts are those in which the reader would assume an incorrect definition from the words surrounding the target or unknown word. For example, in the following sentence, readers might assume that an *anchorite* was someone who liked being around people and not that it means a person who lives in seclusion usually for religious reasons. The words around the unknown word convey a different message and are therefore misdirective.

> It's hard to imagine James was an anchorite. He's so full of life and love of people. He often is the last to leave a party.

Alternatively, a *nondirective* context clue is of little or no assistance to the reader. These clues fail to help the reader make meaning. For most readers unfamiliar with the terms *loquacious*, *melancholy*, and *pococurante*, the context doesn't help the reader understand the words being used to describe Jessica in the following example.

> Jessica seems to change based on her environment and whom she's with. She can be loquacious, melancholy, or pococurante.

General context clues provide readers with some information, but not a level of detail that would allow them to identify specific nuances or connotations of the words. Readers of the following sentence have a sense that *ambled* means to have moved slowly. Readers may not understand that the word more specifically connotes an unhurried or leisurely walk and that the author is playing with the word because *ambled* is also used to describe an easy gait, especially that of a horse.

> Justin ambled to the stable, not at all in a hurry to get himself on another horse.

And finally, the type of context clue that really helps the reader is a *directive* one. These clues provide readers with information that they can use to determine the word's meaning, and even the nuances of the word, from reading around the word. Consider the word *gauche* in the following sentence. Readers unfamiliar with the word will easily sense that the writer has chosen a word that conveys distaste and a lack of social polish.

> Joan's behavior, licking the spoon, telling toilet jokes, and criticizing the food during dinner, is tacky, crude, and even vulgar, to the point of being gauche.

Given that there are so many context clues that don't work, it seems reasonable to add a note of caution about spending too much class time trying to teach students to use context clues. Or rather, we must balance it with teaching them how to determine *if* the context clues are going to help them; sometimes our weaker students get trapped in erroneous meanings because they think context clues will always work. When you consider that our students are reading widely, seeing all kinds of words in different contexts, then it becomes clear we have to teach them how to muddle through all kinds of idiosyncratic contexts, some helpful, some not. As Beck, McKeown, and Kucan (2002) asserted, we don't want students to learn words only *in* context; we need to teach them how to learn words *from* context. There are a number of texts, especially informational texts and textbooks, in which authors purposefully embed words in context to help readers comprehend.

Teacher modeling solving words

As such, the use of context clues should not be left to chance and this is where teacher modeling comes in. Modeling the five ways in which authors provide context clues helps students develop their skill in using context to discover words and their meanings.

1. *Definition or Explanation Clues*: The most obvious clue occurs when the author explains the word immediately after its use. For example:

   Access to clean water would ameliorate, and improve upon, living conditions within the village.

2. *Restatement or Synonym Clues*: Sometimes authors provide a restatement or synonym of the harder word. For example:

   Access to clean water would ameliorate living conditions within the village such that life would be tolerable for the people who live there.

3. *Contrast or Antonym Clues*: Some clues provide a contrast for the target word such that readers can infer the word's meaning while reading. For example:

> Access to clean water would ameliorate living conditions within the village whereas continued reliance on a polluted river will exacerbate a bad situation.

4. *Inference or General Context Clues*: Sometimes a word or phrase is not immediately clarified within the sentence. Relationships, while not directly apparent, are inferred or implied. The reader must look for clues before or after the sentence in which the word is used. For example:

> Access to clean water would ameliorate living conditions within the village. Clean water would make life tolerable as residents could focus on other pressing needs such as finding food and shelter.

5. *Punctuation Clues*: Readers can also use punctuation and font style to infer word meanings. Quotation marks (showing the word has a special meaning), dashes, parentheses or brackets (enclosing a definition), and italics (showing the word will be defined) all help readers determine what the word means in the given context.

> Access to clean water would ameliorate—make tolerable—living conditions within the village.

Let's consider the impact that teacher modeling of context clues has had on Amanda. We've already seen how her teacher Ms. Tran defined unfamiliar vocabulary while solving a problem and reading from a text. Of course teacher modeling with texts is not limited to vocabulary work; teachers also model comprehension and text structures. In this book, however, we focus on the vocabulary examples that teachers provide their students. It's important to note that the teachers quoted in this book did not limit their modeling to vocabulary; they also explained their use of comprehension strategies. For example, Amanda's teacher read aloud and modeled during language arts from *The Incredible Journey* (Burnford 1960):

> It would have been impossible to find three more contented animals that night. They lay curled closely together in a hollow filled with sweet-scented needles, under an aged, spreading balsam tree, near the banks of the stream. The old dog had his beloved cat, warm and purring between his paws again, and he snored in deep contentment. The young dog, their gently worried leader, had found his charge again. He could continue with a lighter heart. (101)

Pausing, the teacher commented, "I appreciate how the author reminded me about the word *contented*. I know from this sentence that she's using the word to mean that the animals are satisfied with the way things are right now. They're not quite happy, but they're also not scared. I have this image in my mind that they're all safe again and that they'll continue the journey after they have a little rest."

Focus on English Language Learners

Idioms and colloquial sayings can be difficult for students new to the language. The phrase *a lighter heart* in this passage is a good example. Model your understanding of idioms when they occur, so as to dispel misunderstandings, in this case about the weight of the heart!

During science, Amanda's teacher read aloud from the text *Extreme Weather* (Farndon 2007), which was projected onto a screen by a document camera. She noticed the word *hailstones* and read aloud the passage that explained them. In doing so, she pointed out the way that the author defined *hailstones* in the text.

> Thunderclouds don't just rain down drops of water. They drop balls of solid ice called hailstones, too. They are typically as a large as peas, but sometimes as large as apples. Hailstones form in thunderclouds because the clouds are so tall that the upper levels are very cold, and so turbulent that they can hold an ice ball aloft. (39)

Following the reading, Ms. Tran noted her appreciation that the author "helped out by very clearly explaining the word *hailstones*." She told the class, "I'm sure that I could have taken a guess by looking inside the word. I know what hail is, we have that, and I know what stones or rocks are, but the context helped me realize that there weren't really small rocks in the hail, but rather they were larger pieces of hail that form specifically in thunderclouds."

It's important for teachers to point out when context clues fail to help the reader. While reading Al Gore's (2007) book *An Inconvenient Truth*, Amanda's integrated arts and sciences (special rotation) teacher noted that sometimes context clues fail. Here's the passage from the text:

The documentary film *March of the Penguins* was a surprise hit in 2005. However, the movie neglected to point out that the population of emperor penguins is thinning.

Since the 1970s, the penguins' neighborhood has become increasingly warm. The Southern Ocean experiences natural shifts in weather from one decade to the next, but this warm spell has continued, causing the thinning of sea ice. Less sea ice means fewer krill, the penguins' main food source. Also, the weakened ice is more likely to break apart and drift out to sea, carrying off the young penguin chicks, who often drown.

Is global warming responsible for the thinning of the penguin population? Scientists believe so. (94)

After reading aloud this passage, the teacher paused and wondered aloud about the word *thinning*: "I'm not sure that I'm correct about this. I know that the word *thin* can mean skinny and not fat. That definition works for the ice; it got skinnier and was more likely to break. But I'm not sure that it applies to the penguins. First, I see the picture and they don't look thin to me. Second, I'm not sure that the former vice president would care about skinny penguins. I have to find out how else the word *thinning* can be used."

Morphology and Word Parts

In addition to looking outside words for clues about their meaning, students need models of looking inside words to determine meaning. Providing examples of how to use morphology and word parts ensures that students apply this strategy on their own. We're using *morphology* here in the linguistic sense, to mean the smallest meaningful units of language. For example, adding an *-s* to the end of many words adds meaning (more than one), as when *dog* becomes *dogs*. But morphology is more complex than that. Teaching students to look inside words for their morphology and word parts requires a fairly sophisticated knowledge of the language. Figure 3.1 identifies five aspects of morphology and word parts that teachers must be aware of if they are to be able to model this inside-the-word approach to determining word meanings. In addition, Chapter 2 provided a table with the most common suffixes and prefixes (see Figure 2.4).

Component	Definition	Example
Prefix	A word part (affix) added to the beginning of a root or base word to create a new meaning	*hyper-* meaning over, as in *hyperactive*
Suffix	A word part (affix) added to the end of a root or base word to create a new meaning	*-est* meaning comparative, as in *tallest*
Root or base	A morpheme or morphemes to which affixes or other bases may be added	*port* meaning to carry, as in *transportation*
Cognates	Two words having the same ancestral language and meaning	*Rehabilitation* and *rehabilitación* meaning to restore or improve
Word family	A group of words sharing a common phonic element	*Judge, judgment, adjudicate, adjudication*

Figure 3.1 *Morphology and word parts*

Like context clues, word parts don't always illuminate meaning. For example, there are a number of false cognates that result in misunderstandings. Consider, for example, the word *embarrassed*. It sounds a lot like the Spanish word *embarazada*, which means pregnant. You certainly wouldn't want to confuse these two terms! Whereas *religion* (English) and *religión* (Spanish) mean more or less the same thing, *fabric* and *fábrica* do not (*fábrica* means factory). Figure 3.2 contains a sampling of the many common Spanish and English cognates useful in school. Using cognates in modeling serves several purposes: it acknowledges the vocabulary strengths of second-language learners in your classroom and builds the language knowledge of the entire class. If you have students who speak other languages, learn about the cognates that occur in their home languages. There are a number

English	Spanish
action	acción
affection	afección
application	aplicación
circulation	circulación
civilization	civilización
classification	clasificación
direction	dirección
election	elección
elevation	elevación
evaporation	evaporación
fiction	ficción
function	función
identification	identificación
infection	infección
investigation	investigación
multiplication	multiplicación
nutrition	nutrición
position	posición
revolution	revolución

Figure 3.2 *English and Spanish cognates*

of resources on the Internet for cognates in other languages, as well as false cognates, and we encourage you to take a look at them.

One of Amanda's teachers also used morphology and word parts—inside-the-word strategies—while modeling. Remember the teacher who was reading aloud from Al Gore's book? When he got to page 120, on which the words *destructive* and *deterioration* occur, he said, "*De-* is an interesting prefix. It means from, down, and away and generally suggests a reversal or removal. That helps me understand the word *destructive*—things being deconstructed, destroyed. It also helps me understand *deterioration*. I know that the root, *-terior*, is related to a geographical area like *territory* and also words like *posterior* and *anterior*, meaning locations. I also know that *-tion* is a process or action. So, *deterioration* means that there is a place that is in the process of removal."

In another case, the teacher came across the word *carnivore* while reading and said, "I remember that *carne* is a Spanish word for meat, as in *carne asada*. The suffix *-vore* focuses on eating. So I can easily figure out that a carnivore is a meat eater. That's different from *herbivore*, which I remember because *herb* is a plant. It's also different from *omnivore*. *Omni-* means everything or all, so an omnivore eats both plants and meat."

Sometimes teachers play with the words they are reading simply as a reminder of the process of using word parts and morphology. For example, while reading *George Washington Carver* (Bolden 2008), a teacher read the sentence "The kid [Carver] was a whiz as Aunt Sue's housework helper and a crackerjack at handicrafts, from carving to crocheting" (7). The teacher stopped and said, "Wait just a minute—*crackerjack*—isn't that a candy? But I know the author isn't talking about a box of popcorn here, because it wouldn't make sense. I remember that *crackerjack* is an old-fashioned word that means a boy who is really good at doing something. The author wants to tell us that George was quick and skilled."

Resources

When the first two approaches—context and word parts—fail, teachers model the use of resources. These take readers even further outside the word to determine meaning. Commonly, teachers use peer resources, dictionaries, and the Internet in their modeled quests for figuring out word meanings.

As an example, let's return to the reading of Al Gore's book. When he wasn't sure that his context clues for *thinning* worked, the teacher clearly indicated that he needed more information. Consulting an online dictionary,

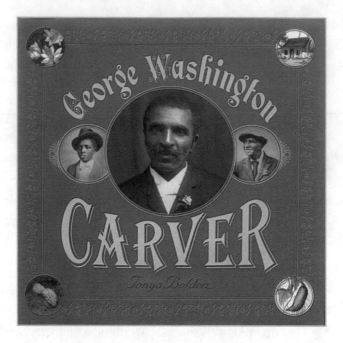

he read aloud a variety of definitions for the word *thinning*. At first, he found a number of definitions that focused on trees and removing some trees to provide growing space for better-quality trees, or removing dead or dying trees to reduce pest problems. Applying this definition aloud for his students also didn't work. He then found a definition that worked—reducing a population—and said to the class, "I think I've got it. Yes, the former vice president would be worried about this, as am I! The ice is getting skinnier, but the penguins are getting fewer and fewer in number. The word *thinning* works in both cases."

Amanda's teacher Ms. Tran modeled using a peer when she called the teacher next door to ask about the word *cirrostratus*, which appears in the sentence "Soon, the blue sky begins to fill up with milky veils of cirrostratus clouds, formed lower down on the front" (Farndon 2007, 36). The teacher next door replied on speaker phone and described a very interesting type of cloud, one that is "almost transparent with a whitish veil of fibrous, almost hairlike, appearance. These clouds usually totally cover the whole sky and often produce a halo phenomenon. These clouds are made of ice crystals and are thin. These clouds are in high altitudes, usually between twenty thousand and forty thousand feet." Thanking her colleague, Ms. Tran added, "I'm never embarrassed to ask a friend about a word. Now I know the word and can help another person—pay it forward, I say. I want to find this kind of cloud and see what else it offers."

■ The Takeaway

Modeling is good first teaching. In fact, our experience and research suggest that it is critical teaching. Simply said, students need—deserve—models they can use in their own reading. That's not to say that modeling is sufficient, in and of itself, as an instructional intervention. Modeling must be part of a larger vocabulary initiative in which students are provided opportunities to build, consolidate, and extend their word knowledge.

Modeling should not take significant amounts of time away from content instruction; vocabulary *is* content instruction. You would be hard-pressed to find an expert lawyer, biologist, or chief financial officer who did not know the words of his or her discipline. Our classrooms would become much better places of learning if we could discontinue the false dichotomy between content and literacy. Using words is how experts across disciplines communicate with one another. Our job as teachers is to welcome students into these conversations.

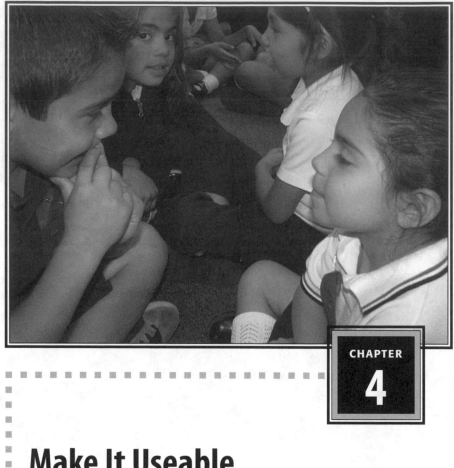

Make It Useable

■ Harnessing the Power of Peer Conversations

VOCABULARY DOESN'T EXIST ONLY AS A SKILL to be tested through multiple-choice items. It is a dynamic aspect of our daily speech, and it helps define how others perceive us. Vocabulary can work against us—those who are too wordy are called *verbose*, while others who lack the verbiage to express themselves clearly are labeled as *inarticulate*. Our speech differs from written language as well. It is punctuated with social markers that reveal our cultural and class origins, our gender, as well as our experiences. Clichés and colloquial expressions, the presence or absence of profanity, even the extent to which we ask questions in a conversation disclose our identity to others. Our relative ability to use vocabulary with precision in conversation is not something that is limited to the school day; we carry our vocabulary with us every moment of our lives.

The language of young children gives us insight into vocabulary development. A toddler who has just learned *dog* labels every four-legged beast this way, be it cat, horse, or elephant. Over time, he acquires more labels and can discern the difference between a dog and a cat. Still later, he possesses the vocabulary of *beagle* and *poodle*. If he grows up to be a dog breeder, he'll correctly identify a Rhodesian ridgeback and a Portuguese water dog.

There's something happening to fuel this development, something that cannot be forgotten in the classroom: Subject area vocabulary development doesn't come about only through listening. Yes, listening is important (as we discussed in the previous chapter). But listening is only one side; speaking is the other. To develop language, the child must engage in conversation with others who shape his understanding of concepts, correct his errors, and give him new labels to use. The vocabulary he develops over time comes in part from the opportunities he has to use vocabulary in spoken language. He then carries the oral language awareness into his reading and writing experiences.

■ The Evidence on Oral Language and Vocabulary Development

Now, for the bad news: Our teaching doesn't reflect what we know both intuitively and through the research about the benefits of talking to learn. More than two decades ago, Cazden (1986) noted that the discourse in most classrooms is dominated by teacher-led discussions that limit participation to a handful of students. Not much has changed since then.

We want to be clear here: Discourse is great when it's a true, classwide exchange. It's a vital element to content learning, as evidenced by the national standards in nearly every subject. What's askew is that in most classrooms the teacher *dominates* the spoken language, asks questions occasionally, and is answered by the same few students (Cazden 2001). So much potential language development and academic development are lost in this unfortunate state of affairs, for oral language development and vocabulary acquisition are strongly linked. One study found that elementary students taught to use heuristic vocabulary in their work with one another improved in their mathematical learning and ability to solve word problems, and the effect was even greater for lower-achieving students (Hohn and Frey 2002). (Here's a bit of vocabulary development: *heuristics* in math are problem-solving approaches such as *make a graph*, *confirm the prediction*, and *keep track of calculations*.)

Importantly, instruction included teacher modeling and collaborative learning using vocabulary. For example, the researchers described how a fourth-grade teacher modeled her use of a heuristic called SOLVED (state, options, link, visualize, execute, do look back) to solve this word problem: The Statue of Liberty stands on a square base. What is the perimeter?

> Perimeter means how far it is all the way around an area. I have to figure out how far it is all the way around the statue. If I start at one point, and go all the way around it until I get back I will know it [*state*]. Since it's a square, I could add all four sides up or multiply one side by four [*options*]—I remember I did a problem like this last week when we measured our bedrooms, but it wasn't square [*link*]. I could draw a picture, but I know what a square looks like [*visualize*]. I am ready to do the math now—I'll multiply 4×65 [*execute*] = 260. That looks right but to check I'll add up the four sides. Still 260. All right! [*do look back*]. (375)

After the teacher modeled, the students worked together with a partner to solve similar word problems using the heuristic and then explain their thinking using the mathematical vocabulary learned. For example, students said:

- "I remembered to multiply by 2."

- "I knew I should look back over my work."

- "I knew I should put the times on a clock face that I drew." (379)

In another study, Pérez (1996) investigated the language gains made by English language learners in a second-grade classroom that featured small-group discussion and instructional conversations. The teacher front-loaded specific vocabulary for them to use (*measure*, *experiment*, *solution*, *observe*, and *results*). Importantly, the students exhibited higher levels of science and math vocabulary and concepts, and they improved in essential social skills like turn taking. It seems that small-group oral language activities that target vocabulary development are useful.

But conversations involving subject area vocabulary don't just break out in the classroom, whether it be among the whole class or small groups. Students have to be taught to have these conversations. And you have to create a culture in the classroom where pursuing word meanings is fun and it's OK to be in the dark about a word. Let students know when you didn't know a word that you came across in your reading outside of school, and let students know you love it when they speak up about a word they don't know. Celebrate it and pursue the answer together right on the spot if at all possible. And when you can, invite English language learners to provide insights about a vocabulary word's equivalent in their native languages.

Now, let's consider the characteristics of productive group work.

■ Characteristics of Productive Group Work

As you know, fostering meaningful work between partners or in small groups is more complicated than simply throwing students together and assigning them a task. It is useful to consider these characteristics of effective peer learning (Johnson, Johnson, and Smith 1991).

- *Positive Interdependence*: The activity should necessarily require the participation and contribution of all members of the group and be one that cannot be done by one member. Lack of participation by any member would diminish the likelihood that the task could be completed successfully.

- *Face-to-Face Interaction*: Never underestimate the power of personal connections between students, especially when the intent is in the development of language. Communicators need face-to-face interaction in order to communicate.

- *Individual and Group Accountability*: This is undoubtedly the most common complaint among teachers and students when group assignments are mentioned. The solution is an easy one but is usually overlooked. Every member needs to be held individually accountable. A group grade in the absence of individual accountability is a surefire recipe for unrest. Our solution? Require all participants to use different ink colors and sign their names accordingly. The evidence of everyone's contribution is instantly apparent.

- *Interpersonal and Small-Group Skills*: Students don't inherently know how to work well with one another. Establish your rules of engagement and teach them. Our rules include the following:
  - Listen as an ally.
  - There is value in every voice.
  - If you have a disagreement, try to solve it together.
  - If you can't resolve it, talk to the teacher.

- *Group Processing*: Students need time to discuss their work together. In a busy classroom, it's easy to push this component aside. Make a habit of building a

Collaborative writing

few minutes into the end of the activity to allow participants to discuss the process they used.

■ Three Tips for Successful Peer Interactions

We always believe in stacking the deck in the favor of the teacher, and peer collaboration activities are no exception. We have found that when we are clear on the purpose of the activity, when we are deliberate in varying the vocabulary enrichment activities, and when we integrate them into content learning, the success rate accelerates.

Tip 1: Provide Students with a Purpose Statement

Most children are sensitive to busywork. The moment they decide that you've given them a task to keep them busy and buy yourself some peace, you're going to have some understandable civil disobedience—the classroom will get noisier as more students get off task. But when you establish a clear purpose with them and link it to interesting content, they'll get on board. This is different from giving directions, which merely list a sequence of steps. Purpose provides students with a model of metacognition so that they recognize a path to learning. In our many visits to classrooms, we have found that establishing a clear purpose is the most neglected instructional design element. We often ask students a simple question: "How do you know when you're done?" If the answer is "When the teacher tells me" or "When it's time for recess," we know that no clear purpose has been established for that learner.

Literally write a purpose statement for your students that includes these three components: First, tell them the *outcome* ("By the end of this activity, you and your partner should be able to identify the phases of the moon."). Second, tell them how the task relates to their *content mastery* ("This will help you to be able to describe how the earth, sun, and moon move through phases."). Third, tell them how they will *measure success* ("You'll know you've done this correctly when you are able to explain the differences to one another without using the graphic organizer you've developed."). We've developed a habit over the years of posting the purpose on the board as well as saying it orally.

Focus on English Language Learners

Students who are learning English benefit greatly from purpose statements that focus their learning on both the content and language use. Encourage personalization by having students restate content and language purposes using "I" statements, such as "I will tell my partner about the phases of the moon."

Tip 2: Remember That Variety Is the Spice of Life

Variety is especially important when it comes to vocabulary development. Students satiate quickly on any one particular vocabulary activity, so we've found it helpful to get into the mind-set of offering up a few different types of peer activities each week. Graphic organizers are great, but not if they are used five days a week. It is a fine balance between establishing habits of work and allowing students to habituate on too few vocabulary activities. Rotating effective vocabulary learning strategies, such as the ones outlined in this book, will ensure that students remain focused on the instruction provided.

**Tip 3:
Integrate
Vocabulary
Activities into
the Content
Flow**

As much as possible, avoid activities that isolate vocabulary from the conceptual understandings of the unit of study. The goal of any activity should center on the necessary use of the vocabulary to complete the task. You won't find activities in this book that have students endlessly looking up dictionary definitions and mindlessly copying them onto worksheets. Nor do we ask students to write contrived sentences containing targeted vocabulary words. We learned our lesson the hard way years ago when we received this assignment from Antonio based on his reading of *The Giver* (Lowry 1993):

1. *Tunic* is a word.

2. *Utopia* is a word.

3. *Inherit* is a word.

And so on—you get the idea. Choose activities for peer interaction that rely on the verbal and written use of vocabulary that is contextually bound. Words serve as the proxy for a multitude of concepts and ideas. You'll find that both vocabulary and content knowledge are built together, as they are an expression of both.

■ Speaking Our Way to Deeper Understandings

As we know, social interaction is key to learning, and students who are paired in subject area conversations scaffold each other's understanding. The goal of the peer interaction activities we describe is to get students to integrate Tier 2 and Tier 3 vocabulary into their spoken communication. Think of this as verbal composition; the likelihood that students will use this vocabulary in written work increases as they become more comfortable with the syntactical (grammar) and semantic (meaning) demands. Of course, the conversations that students are having with one another should contain the words you've selected. In addition, students will likely need to draw on their developing knowledge of specialized vocabulary to engage in conversations with their peers.

**Noticing and
Clarifying
Understanding**

*Partner
Discussions*

Discussions with a partner are ideal for creating immediate opportunities for students to integrate new vocabulary into their oral language. In addition, they are easy to implement because they don't require materials or the movement of furniture. The most well-known partner technique is *think-pair-share* (Lyman 1987), first conceived as a cooperative learning arrangement but quickly recognized for its value in allowing students to notice what they know and don't know and to seek clarification. This activity is implemented in three parts, beginning with a question that is posed to students ("What are some of the differences between eastern woodland Native American villages and the ones in the plains?"). Students are instructed to think about their response for a minute or two (a timer works best), then share their thoughts with another student ("The tribes in the east lived in longhouses and wigwams, and they built their villages to last a long time. Some of the Plains tribes moved a lot to follow the bison they hunted."). Finally, the teacher elicits responses from the class ("Let's hear from some of you about the differences between eastern woodland tribes and those on the plains."). Short or incomplete responses can be scaffolded by the teacher to ensure that subject area vocabulary is used in front of the entire class. For example, when Jerrod reported that "they [Plains Indians] moved a lot," his teacher scaffolded the response for the whole class by saying, "Yes, some of the Plains Native Americans were nomadic, meaning that they moved from one place to another."

Another worthwhile partner discussion activity is *turn to your partner and . . .*, often recorded in teacher lesson plan notebooks as *TTYPA*. As with think-pair-share, a well-crafted question will bring forth richer responses, so we are sure to plan questions in advance. These are great for planting vocabulary within group discussions. For instance, the teacher continued the conversation about Native American tribes by saying, "Turn to your partner and explain why many Plains tribes were nomadic. Be sure to use that term in your discussion." These prompts lower the risk for some learners who are reluctant to speak in front of the entire class, including some English language learners who may be feeling self-conscious about their language skills. By walking around and listening in on the conversations that partners have, the teacher knows which students use the terms correctly and which students need further instruction.

Small-Group Discussions

Managing groups of three or more gets to be a bit more complicated, so procedures really pay off. A variation of think-pair-share is called *think-pair-square* (Kagan 1989). The first two steps are the same, with students discussing a question in groups of two. On the teacher's signal, the partners then turn to another set of partners to confer. This is an especially useful way to foster discussions among students.

The use of oral composition is good preparation for more formal written work (Dykstra 1994). When students have a chance to make meaning by talking with a peer, they are more likely to have fodder for writing tasks.

Students who struggle with reading often get lost in small-group conversations. There is a temptation for teachers to cluster them together, but this is a mistake. Group conversations provide the kind of language models and interactions with higher-performing students these learners need. There are two ways we support them in these groups: First, we give each student in the group a task card so that each child has a specific role or topic for which he is responsible. Second, we do a lot of fishbowl-style modeling of what it means to be a productive group member, so that all children learn to take care of each other's participation in the group. We model and debrief as a class about good listening skills, ways to bring in students who aren't talking, and specific phrases that help children to piggyback on one another's ideas ("I agree with what *x* said, and I'd like to add . . ." or "I had a different way of thinking about that. . . ."). There is nothing more rewarding than seeing—after weeks and months of practice—children of varying reading levels participating on the equal playing field of small-group discussion. The stronger readers end up mentoring the less able ones, and everyone has learned how to *facilitate* group conversation.

For example, the group of students talking about Native Americans was asked to summarize their understanding following the conversation. Martha wrote the following after the group conversation, which provides evidence of key vocabulary terms that were intentionally taught:

> The Eastern woodland tribes had villages of longhouses or wigwams. They traded with other villages. Some of the villages were close together. The Plains Native Americans lived in a bigger space called the Plains. They followed buffalo [*sic*] and they were nomads.

Group conversations can be useful for sharing information read individually by members of the group. In addition, the opportunity to retell reinforces the use of new vocabulary and concepts. The *jigsaw* method of small-group discussion is completed in two stages (Aronson et al. 1978). Students work first in an expert group of four members, with the shared goal of understanding a section of text. They read and discuss the main ideas and the supporting details with one another, asking questions to clarify their understanding. Once the expert group is satisfied that they are comfortable with the information and can report it accurately, each student returns to a second group of four, called the home group. The home group is composed of a representative from each expert group. Together, each of the four members of the heterogeneous home group shares the information she learned in her expert group. Members of the home group take notes and ask questions, seeking to synthesize the information. For example, fourth-grade teacher Mr. Bristow established four expert groups to participate in a jigsaw discussion of the following concepts:

- herbivores

- carnivores

- omnivores

- decomposers

Students worked in groups of four to read and discuss information about these producers and consumers in the food chain, then returned to a home group of four to share and learn about each type. Mr. Bristow gave each student a note-taking guide called a *conversational roundtable* (Burke 2002) to foster recall (see Figure 4.1). Using the jigsaw process, students received multiple exposures to new vocabulary: reading, questioning and discussion, listening, retelling, and writing. Of course, they had to use both inside-the-word and outside-the-word strategies that had been modeled for them by their teacher in figuring out unknown words.

Student Think-Alouds: Modeling for Peers

In Chapter 3, we made a case for the importance of teachers modeling their thinking for students. Of course students can also think aloud—that is, model—for one another. There is a strong evidence base for the use of peer think-alouds. We know, for example, that student think-alouds improve comprehension (Baumann, Jones, and Seifert-Kessell 1993). We also know that student think-alouds provide peers with alternative models for understanding texts as well as authentic examples of using vocabulary to understand content (Oster 2001; Wilhelm 2001).

Students don't automatically know how to think aloud or even what to think aloud. Before asking students to engage in think-alouds, you must show them how. This instruction should provide examples and nonexamples of the type of talk expected during partner or small-group think-alouds.

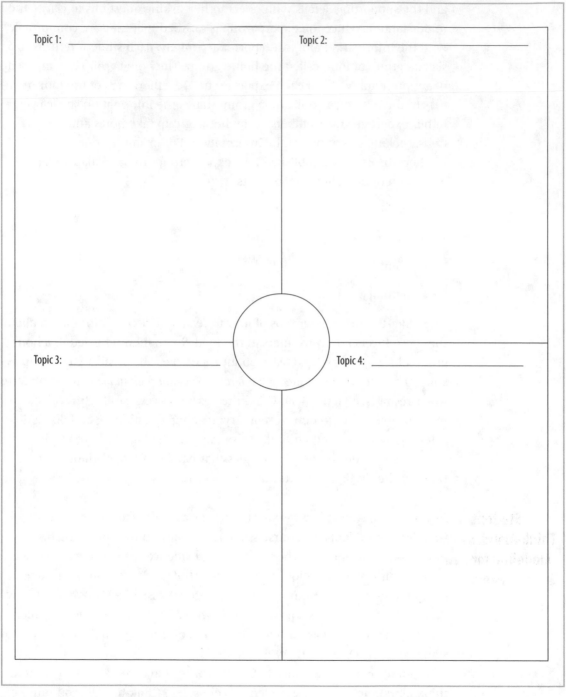

Topic 1: _____

Topic 2: _____

Topic 3: _____

Topic 4: _____

From *Learning Words Inside and Out*. Portsmouth, NH: Heinemann. © 2002 by Jim Burke from *Tools for Thought*. Portsmouth, NH: Heinemann.

Figure 4.1 *Conversational roundtable*

In our experience, students need to be reminded that these are not discussion groups (the previously discussed approach), nor are they read-alouds. In fact, we insist that students do not read the text aloud. They read the text individually in small chunks, and then one student shares his thinking with the group. The students continue this process until they've completed the text. In doing so, the group members have opportunities to listen in on each other's thinking.

Naturally, student think-alouds can be used in any content area. It's easy to imagine a small group of students each sharing their thinking as they read about plant life cycles, insects, westward expansion, or picture book author-illustrator Eric Carle. But as a more detailed example, let's focus on Ms. Kelso's fifth-grade classroom. The students are focused on literary devices and point of view. Groups of students are reading different texts and Ms. Kelso is joining different groups to listen in on their think-alouds. She knows which students she really wants to hear, as this is part of her formative assessment system. By noticing how students think about texts, and the vocabulary they use to explain their thinking, Ms. Kelso knows which of her students need additional instruction and which of her students are meeting standards and expectations for the grade level.

Ms. Kelso joins the group reading *Sarah, Plain and Tall* (MacLachlan 1985). It's Marshall's turn to share his thinking. Marshall has difficulty expressing himself in large groups and Ms. Kelso knows that this practice and the feedback he receives from his peers will help him become more comfortable speaking in front of others. The group members have read the first two chapters of the text in advance. Marshall starts talking:

> I think that this is third-person point of view because the narrator seems to know a lot about the characters. The first chapter starts with Caleb talking about his mom, like . . . what do you call when you see the past? [*Pauses*] A flashback, yeah, but more wanting to remember her. His mom died when he was one day old. When I first started reading, I thought they were happy but then it's more sad, like depressing. But there's also sarcasm—Anna is sarcastic with him because she has to tell the story lots of times. It's like my little sister. I have to answer the same question over and over.

Marshall continues, sharing his thinking for a few more minutes before turning to the group for comments. Tricia, a member of the group, agrees that the mood changes. "I like that you picked the word *sarcasm*. I think that the author tries to have a tone in the book because you can just see in your

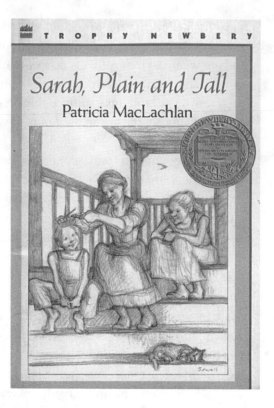

mind how she would answer Caleb's questions. I also think that it's sad when she goes outside to remember the day her mom died."

After a short discussion in which members of the group have a chance to ask Marshall questions and comment on his thinking, they individually read the next chapter. Now it's Adam's turn to share his thinking. Ms. Kelso moves to the next group, pleased with the discussion she has witnessed. She notes that her students were thinking like literary critics, as evidenced by their use of the technical language she had introduced. She is also pleased that her students were able to ask questions, civilly, of one another about their thinking using specialized vocabulary.

The success of this peer work was based on a lot of practice. Ms. Kelso had modeled these respectful behaviors many times, and she had conducted think-alouds of her process of solving unknown words by using inside-the-word and outside-the-word strategies. Through good old trial and error, she'd come to realize that students did their best work when she explicitly required they use specific academic language in their conversations with one another. Earlier, she left it to chance and hoped the words would bubble up naturally, but they hadn't. As with each of these activities, you'll find your own ways of making them work well for your particular students.

Reciprocal Teaching: Structured Conversations

Reciprocal teaching is a peer discussion technique that requires students to use four specific comprehension strategies in conversations with their peers (Palincsar 1987):

1. *Summarizing*: The goal of the summary is to identify the major points presented by the author. The person responsible for summarizing the text reads the text with the purpose of getting the gist.

2. *Questioning*: The person responsible for this component identifies specific questions that the group can talk about. Questions can range from those found right in the text to those that require conjecture and personal connections.

3. *Clarifying*: The person responsible for clarifying attempts to clear up any confusions that the group has. To start, the clarifier notes words or ideas that might be confusing and asks members of the group for ideas. The clarifier is not expected to have all of the answers but is expected to facilitate the conversation. Of course, other members of the group can ask for clarifications.

4. *Predicting*: The person responsible for predicting makes an educated guess about what might come next in the text. The predictions should be plausible and realistic and should generate interest in reading the next section.

After reading a selection of text, students engage in a discussion. Typically, groups of four students have this conversation so that each student has something to do. One student summarizes, another questions, another clarifies, and the fourth predicts what might come next. During each reading, students take turns and rotate through each of the four comprehension components. The text is chunked or parsed, either by the teacher or by the group of students, and they stop at predetermined times while reading to discuss what they have read. Over time, and with practice, students begin to incorporate these four comprehension strategies into their independent reading (Oczkus 2003).

As you've probably figured out by now, we're interested specifically in the impact that this instructional routine has on subject matter word learning. Imagine a group of students engaged in a structured conversation such as one based on reciprocal teaching. One of the components is clarifying, so students naturally talk about words that are confusing to them. Most often, they clarify Tier 3 words using either inside-the-word or outside-the-word strategies. That's the obvious effect that reciprocal teaching has on word knowledge. But think about the other components. When students summarize, question, and predict, they have to use all kinds of vocabulary: general, specialized, and technical. To talk about something they're reading requires that they use the words provided in the reading. Thus this instructional routine is one more way that teachers can ensure students *use the words* and build their vocabulary knowledge.

Consider the opportunities reciprocal teaching provided students in the study of insects. We had a chance to observe a group of four students read an informational website about insect metamorphosis. During the reading and the reciprocal teaching discussion they had, the students in this group experimented with a number of new ideas and new words. Some of the words they wrestled with were specialized terms. For example, *creature* is used generically, whereas students often think of creatures as scary monsters. The text also uses the term *order* in a scientific way, as in groupings, and uses *matter* to describe something with mass that occupies space.

In addition to the specialized words, the students in this group used a number of technical, content-specific words, including *thorax, abdomen,* and *exoskeleton*. As evidence that they used these words in their discussions, consider the following excerpts from their conversation about the reading:

Bradley: But I thought a spider was in the order of insects because my mom always says, "Kill that bug."

Micha: But they can't be insects. They are a different creature because they don't meet the conditions, like it says here [*points to text*].

Janae: Yeah, insects gotta only have six legs and spiders have eight.

Bradley: And they don't have the three body parts, only two. They don't have the thorax or abdomen. Do spiders have an exoskeleton?

As we have noted, structuring conversations such that students build their vocabulary use is critical. If these students had simply been asked to define these terms, in the absence of an interesting reading and a peer discussion, we're not sure that they would have incorporated this information. Again, it's about the opportunities we provide students to use the words of the discipline.

■ Seeing Our Way to Deeper Understandings in the Subject Areas

Content vocabulary learning is strengthened through visual displays of information. These have been found to be particularly effective when it is the student, rather than the teacher, who is generating the visual display (McCagg and Dansereau 1991). Sometimes called *knowledge mapping*, these strategies allow students to position vocabulary in physical space in order to represent conceptual relationships. However, students do not have time to create visual representations of all the words they need to know. Word selection is critical. Choosing words that are worth it, as discussed in Chapter 2, is one of the most important things teachers can do in preparation for building subject area vocabulary learning with visuals.

Word Maps: Making Connections Visible

There is a significant body of research that suggests that graphic organizers facilitate student learning (Ives 2007; Robinson 1998). Explanations for this increased learning focus on the fact that graphic organizers provide learners with visual representations of the content at hand (Fisher 2001). Graphic organizers also help students become more active readers in that they have a task to complete as they read (Alvermann and Boothby 1982). When graphic organizers correspond with the text structure, they help students clarify connections and relationships between concepts and ideas found in their reading (Fisher and Frey 2007). As a profession, we've known this for a long time.

But our focus here is on word learning. And unfortunately, the ways that graphic organizers are often used actually impede vocabulary development. Graphic organizers offer an opportunity for students to think, in words, about the content. They provide students a way of organizing information, again in words and sometimes images, in a way that helps them understand and remember. When well-meaning teachers simply copy a blackline master of a graphic organizer, the teacher, and not the student, is doing the thinking. When well-meaning teachers who have heard that graphic organizers are helpful complete a graphic organizer on the overhead while members of the whole class add words, an opportunity is lost.

Looking through the lens of subject area word learning, we can see that the power of graphic organizers lies in their ability to facilitate conversations among students. Students need to be taught a number of types of graphic organizers and then be encouraged to use an appropriate graphic organizer to visually represent information (again, almost always with words). A list of common graphic organizers can be found in Figure 4.2. Additional examples can be found at www.edhelper.com.

To appreciate graphic organizers in action, let's turn to a discussion a group of second graders had about plant and animal life cycles. The group had selected a vocabulary word map (e.g., Rosenbaum 2001), which is

Type	Description	Example
Venn	Overlapping circles that illustrate similarities and differences between two concepts	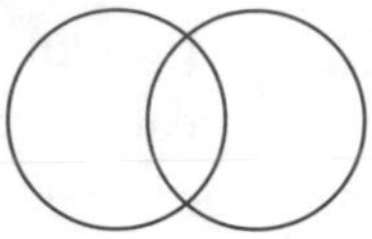
Web	Central word or phrase linked to supporting labels, concepts, and ideas	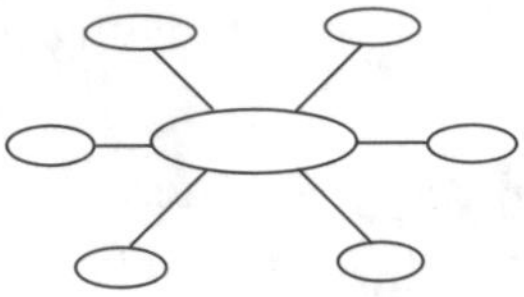
Sequence/process	Shows series of steps	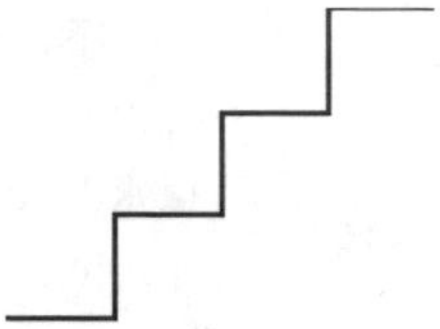
Chart/matrix	Rows and columns in table format that shows relationships vertically and horizontally	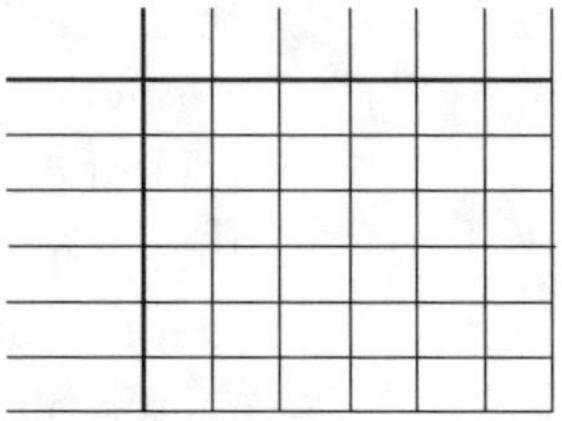
T-chart	Two-column table for grouping ideas into categories	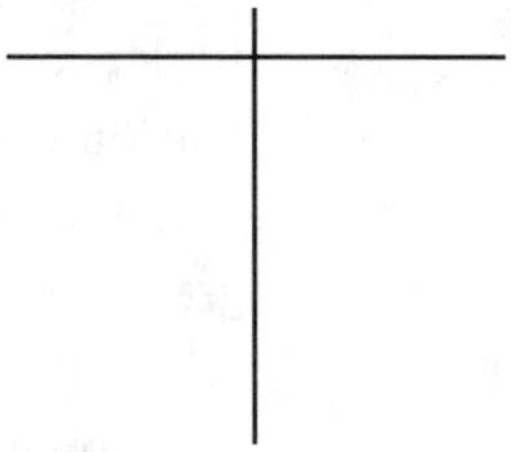
KWL chart	Three-column chart for recording what is *known* about a topic, what students *want* to learn, and later, what they have *learned* about the topic	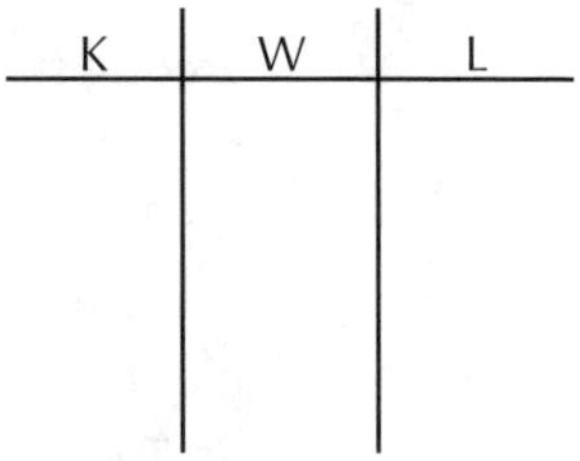

Figure 4.2 *Common graphic organizers*

especially effective for helping students engage with and think about new terms or concepts in specific ways. (Other small groups used a time line and a compare-and-contrast chart. The key is the conversation that occurs as students complete the task, for it's here that subject area vocabulary gets bandied about and refined by peers.)

The group using a vocabulary word map was focused on the term *offspring*. Here are a few of the comments made by group members as they constructed their map:

Jeremy: Ms. Brown said that the babies look like their parents, but the baby chickens don't look like their mom.

Brian: But they do when they grow up. They have to get bigger first. The offspring grow up to look like the adults.

Natalie: Just like the puppies and kitties have to grow up to look like their mommy. Well not exactly like them. But kinda like them, like a mix of the mom and the dad.

Hunter: When my dog had babies, some looked more like her but some looked like the dad.

Brian: But they all looked like dogs, right? They didn't look like cats because dogs can't have baby cats. That's the wrong offspring.

Natalie: But that's funny. What if a chicken had a baby cat!

Brian: That's crazy! It can't happen that way.

Natalie: I know, but it's funny to me.

In this brief excerpt, it's striking to see how this group of students used general, specialized, and technical vocabulary, isn't it? Notice how they incorporated the words they'd met in texts and from their teacher into their conversations. They clarified ideas and made connections with one another as they negotiated the task of creating the vocabulary word map. Again, the power is in the conversation, not the paper. Students need multiple opportunities such as this to build their vocabulary knowledge with their peers.

Semantic Feature Analysis: Exploring Relationships Between Words

Another, very specific, type of graphic organizer is a semantic feature analysis. It's a matrix of sorts. Using this tool, students can examine related concepts (words) and make distinctions between them. We know that semantic feature analyses facilitate comprehension and engagement (Pittelman et al. 1991). We also know that this tool is a powerful way for engaging students in world learning (Stahl 1999). In working on the distinction between words, ideas, and categories, students use both specialized and technical vocabulary. The key for us is to get students talking about the categories, persuading one another whether or not a characteristic applies.

It's easy to see the value of students building their vocabulary learning using semantic feature analysis by visiting Javier Trujillo's third-grade class while students are studying types of environments such as oceans, deserts, tundra, forests, grasslands, and wetlands. Mr. Trujillo focuses a great deal of instructional attention on environments and the plants and animals that survive in each environment. At one point in this unit of study, students complete a semantic feature analysis chart comparing environments. Mr. Trujillo said, "They really need to see the differences between the various types of environments. I have them talking about the differences. And I want them to record the differences for later reference. Along the way, I want students to become comfortable with the scientific vocabulary."

Using the tool in Figure 4.3, students meet in groups and debate the answers with one another. Here's a part of one group's conversation:

Jesse: What does it mean, tundra?

Andy: It's like the Arctic, where the polar bears live.

Jesse: So there are no trees there, right?

Component	Oceans	Deserts	Tundra	Forest	Grasslands	Wetlands
Trees	O	O	—	✚	✚	✚
Water supply	✚	—	—	—	✚	✚
Hot temperature	O	✚	—	—	—	—
Food supply	✚	—	—	✚	✚	✚

Key:

O (none)

— (not a lot)

✚ (a lot)

Figure 4.3 *Semantic feature analysis on environments*

Andy: Right, and probably not a lot of food for people.

Ruth: But there's water, lots of cold water.

It's clear that these students need continued work on their vocabulary relative to biomes. It's also obvious that they have strategies for figuring out the ways in which these words work. They use the technical terms with one another and figure out the task at hand. They also trust one another and engage in interesting discussions about the ideas of biology. Mr. Trujillo knows that his students will come to understand the vocabulary as they use it. He listens in on group conversations so he knows which words are still difficult for his students. With this information in mind, Mr. Trujillo can plan subsequent opportunities for interaction as well as individual activities for his students.

Concept Circles: Understanding Attributes

To know a word is to know its attributes. You may recall the contentious debate in 2006 among members of the International Astronomical Union as they argued, and eventually voted on, a definition of *planet*. We'd like to think that these experts would have agreed long ago about what constitutes a planet, but it turns out that the more you know about something, the more precise the language must be to describe and define it. After all, if it is round, large, and orbits a star, isn't it a planet? It turns out that this definition is simplistic, because it allows for too many objects to be classified as a planet. The experts determined that in order for something to be considered a planet, it also has to possess enough gravity to be able to clear a path for itself in its orbit; in other words, it has to be able to push other debris out of its way through gravity, not just collision.

If we arranged the pre– and post–August 2006 definitions of a planet into concept circles, they would look like Figure 4.4.

Poor little Pluto lost its status as a planet because of this change in definition. While there is still much debate about this definition (particularly because Neptune doesn't completely sweep its orbit; Pluto is in the way), the point here is that knowing the attributes of a word allows us to know the word. Concept circles are a way of representing those attributes visually through knowledge mapping.

Concept circles can be used in a variety of ways. The most obvious are ones that are teacher created, which are necessary for modeling how concept circles are developed and interpreted. Once students are comfortable with the process, allow them to create concept circles in partners or small groups. These student-created concept circles can be collected by the teacher

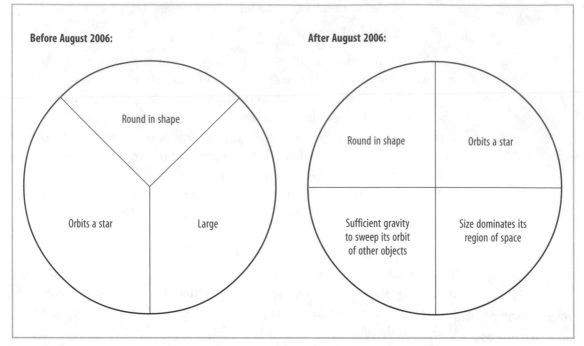

Figure 4.4 *Concept circles of two definitions of* planet

and redistributed to other groups. Choose one of the following conditions for students to apply as they develop original concept circles:

- Player identifies concepts based on attributes.
- Player identifies the incorrect attribute in a concept circle.

Miriam and Beatriz developed a concept circle about geometric shapes. In their discussion about squares, they attempted to identify three attributes that were unique to a square and one that was not (see Figure 4.5 for their work). Once they and their classmates had developed their concept circles, their teacher collected them and had other groups try to figure out the answers. Given the focus on attributes, concept circles are a great way for students to develop their outside-the-word problem-solving skills.

Shades of Meaning: Noticing Subtle Differences Between Words

The subtle differences between related words can be very confusing for students. While they might have a general sense of the difference between *overjoyed* and *ecstatic*, most students would be hard-pressed to define and use these terms in specific ways. In other words, most likely would see these two words as synonyms and not comprehend the differences authors intend when they use one word or the other.

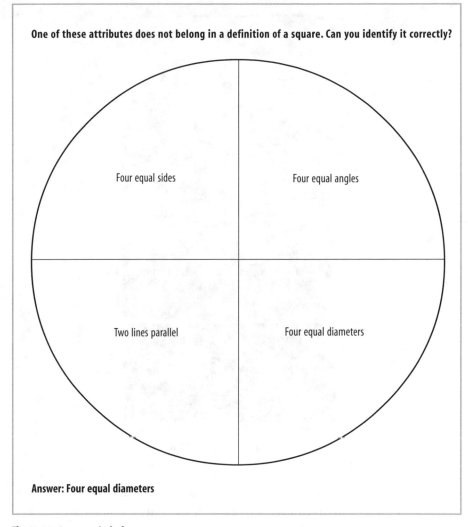

Figure 4.5 *Concept circle for a square*

Goodman (2004) developed the shades-of-meaning strategy as a way to address this need and help students develop their understanding that many words can be organized in gradients of meaning. The shades-of-meaning strategy encourages students to talk about words and organize them along a continuum.

The easiest way to develop students' understanding of the differences between related words is to use paint chips. Most hardware stores will provide you with paint chips for free. Using a paint chip, students identify a continuum of words and then write the words on the colored sections of the paint

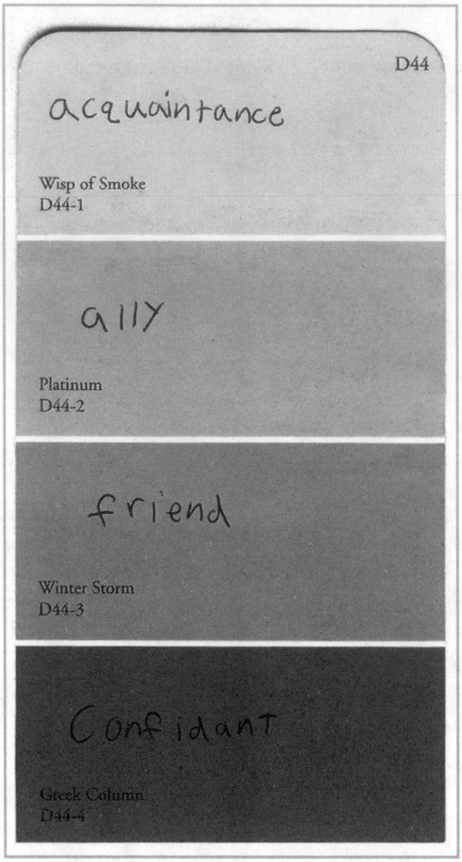

Figure 4.6 *Shades-of-meaning paint chip*

chip. Figure 4.6 contains a sample paint chip showing words related to friendship that a group of students created after reading the book *Owen and Mzee: The True Story of a Remarkable Friendship* (Hatkoff, Hatkoff, and Kahumbu 2006).

As you can imagine, the conversation this group of students had about friendship and the words related to friendship was powerful. During their conversation, students used specialized words to convey their understandings. They also clarified their understanding of the words and provided one another with examples from their own experiences. For example, Mubarik said, "*Ally* means friend, right? Someone who can help you, like provide assistance, like a friend."

Tynesia agreed, but added, "I see a friend as an ally, but I think that an ally doesn't have the depth of a friendship. Friends are there regardless, in any circumstance. Being friends extends beyond being an ally."

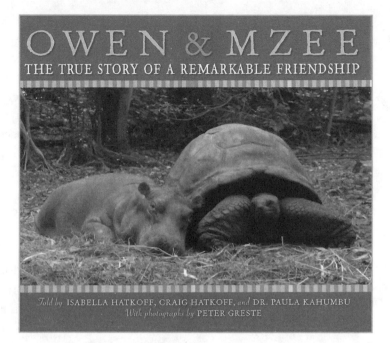

■ Writing Our Way to Deeper Understandings in the Subject Areas

Now we'll focus on peer interaction activities that develop content vocabulary primarily through written language. The overarching goal of these activities is to cause students to integrate Tier 2 and Tier 3 vocabulary into their written communication. This is the traditional composition and we know that the likelihood that students will use this vocabulary in written work increases as they have more opportunities to use vocabulary in their writing. As with the other activities in this chapter, selecting specific vocabulary for use with these strategies is critical. Students simply do not have time to work with words they already know and use. They need to spend time integrating new technical vocabulary and novel uses of specialized vocabulary into their daily writing tasks.

Text Impressions: Making an Impact

Text impressions, also known as story impressions (McGinley and Denner 1987) and semantic impressions (Richek 2005), provide students an opportunity to build their vocabulary as they read a list of words, write a paragraph containing those words, and then discuss the topic with their peers. The key to text impressions is the writing that students do. They have to place the words in context, often demonstrating their knowledge of the definitions, to write the paragraph.

The process for using text impressions is fairly simple. It starts with the teacher identifying key vocabulary words from an upcoming reading or unit of study. The selected words should meet the criteria outlined in Chapter 2 and the list of words should number between ten and twenty. Text impressions are most effective when there is a mix of specialized and technical words. Of course, students will not develop deep knowledge of all of these words from this one activity, but remember that this will not be the only exposure students have to the words. They'll read them or use them later.

Once you have selected the words, arrange the words and phrases vertically with arrows signifying the sequence in which they appear in the text. For example, Figure 4.7 contains a list of words used in a text impression. Students in the class were studying the Arctic region and were about to read a piece of text focused on the Arctic chill (Farndon 2007).

The teacher then introduces the words and phrases, explaining each. Typically, the teacher facilitates a conversation about the words and provides students opportunities to talk about the terms and to ask questions. This generates a great deal of attention for the words. As the conversation comes to an end, students write paragraphs containing the words. Our experience suggests that these paragraphs are best written by partners or small groups. Of course, all of the students don't need to be working on this task at the same time, but they do need to accomplish it at some point in the lesson. Figure 4.8 contains the paragraph written by one of the groups in Ms. Harvey's class.

It's easy to see that the students in this group have a reasonable understanding of many of the vocabulary words, both specialized and technical, that they need to know to read the text. It's also easy to see that their understanding of some of the concepts is limited. For example, they may or may not know what *peeks* means. Similarly, the use of *horizon* is fairly basic and their understanding of the word will likely expand when they read the text and learn specific scientific information about horizons.

When they have all completed their paragraphs, Ms. Harvey has her students share them with the class and discuss their thinking. After this has occurred, students can read the targeted text, looking for the words from the text impression chart. Ms. Harvey asks students to write definitions inferred from the reading on sticky notes when they find the target words so that they can review their group paragraph and write an individual paragraph with more precise meanings for the selected words.

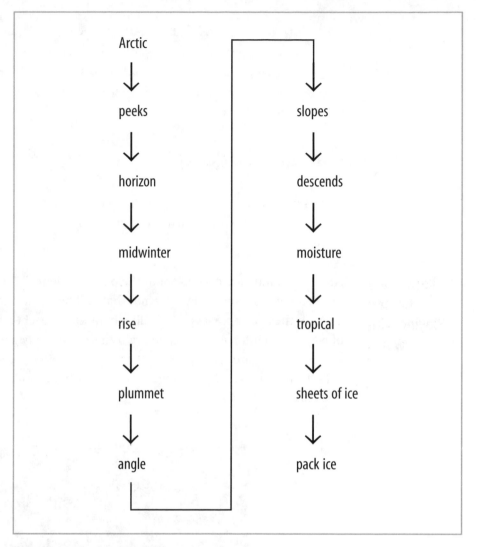

Arctic

↓

peeks

↓

horizon

↓

midwinter

↓

rise

↓

plummet

↓

angle

slopes

↓

descends

↓

moisture

↓

tropical

↓

sheets of ice

↓

pack ice

Figure 4.7 *Words selected for text impression*

Text impressions provide students multiple opportunities to build their word learning. They can use both inside-the-word and outside-the-word strategies to think about word meaning. Inside-the-word strategies are fairly obvious; outside-the-word strategies may not be as obvious. To figure out unknown words, students have to use other words on the list, information presented by the teacher, and data from the class discussion. As such, students build their vocabulary knowledge as they listen to their teacher introduce the words, when they talk about the words, as they write in small

The artic is a very cold place that peeks over the horizon at the top of the world. During the midwinter, the temperature can never rise above 0. Sometimes the temperature can plummet to -50. The angle of the slopes of the mountains in the Arctic don't help. They make it even colder. As the temperature in the Arctic descends, moisture freezes (this isn't tropical!) and sheets of ice become pack ice.

Figure 4.8 *Sample text impression paragraph*

groups using the words, when they read a text containing the words, and finally as they write their own paragraph with enhanced knowledge of the words.

Vocabulary Games: Playing with Words

Ana and Brandy are excited about the day's challenge. They and their classmates are pairing up to devise games that will help one another prepare for a test in their science class. Ms. Willingham, their teacher, has used a variety of games to reinforce key vocabulary terms since the beginning of the year, so her students are well versed in the formats of bingo, *Jeopardy!*, *Who Wants to Be a Millionaire*, *Hollywood Squares*, Balderdash, Scrabble, *Wheel of Fortune*, and *Password*.

The girls are designing a category game based on the old *$25,000 Pyramid* show to help their peers shore up their understanding of nutrition. To pull this off, they have to determine the key understandings in the unit the class completed; these will be the hidden categories on the game board (see Figure 4.9). The players will have to name these categories (e.g., types of whole grains, things to avoid) based on the examples they are given. Brandy and Ana have compiled a list of possible examples for each category, which took quite a bit of discussion, negotiation, and reviewing of the unit. These girls know the examples they offer up to classmates must represent the categories adequately (see Figure 4.10) or the game won't be fair—or fun to play.

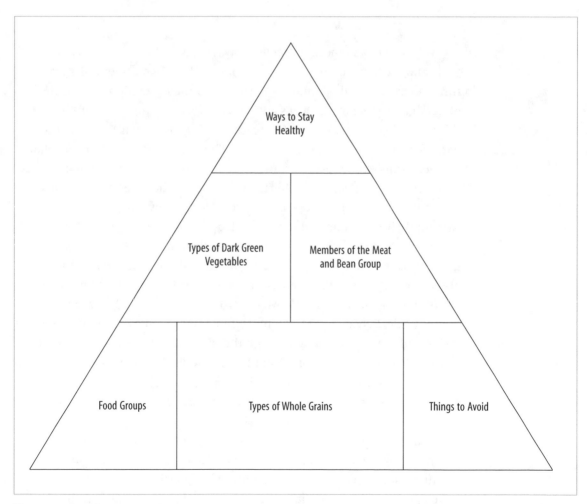

Figure 4.9 *Pyramid game on Ancient Greece*

Food Groups	Whole Grains	Things to Avoid	Dark Green Vegetables	Meat and Beans Group	Ways to Stay Healthy

Grains
Oils
Fruits
Meat and beans
Milk
Vegetables
	Oatmeal
	
	Brown rice
	
	Whole wheat
	  flour
		Oils
		fats
		Refined sugar
		Processed
		  grains
			Broccoli
			Kale
			Spinach
			Romaine
			Collard greens
				Seeds
				Chicken
				Beef
				Fish
				Black beans
				Nuts
					Exercise
					Use the
					  pyramid
					Avoid oils
					  and fats

Figure 4.10 *List of clues for the Pyramid game*

"We need to add more to the list of ways to stay healthy," says Ana.

Brandy returns to the pamphlets from the U.S. Department of Agriculture and adds "avoid oils and fats." They turn their attention back to the list of dark green vegetables. "Let's add romaine," says Brandy. "Everyone thinks that's just for a salad." The teacher, who has been listening in on partner conversations, smiles to herself. The vocabulary development that accrues from a student conversation like this one is the real McCoy; the actual playing of the game is the icing on the cake. She loves hearing the excited tone in students' voices and the confidence they exude when they explain their reasoning and new knowledge.

We conclude this chapter with an example of the use of vocabulary games because we want to emphasize that word learning can be fun. We also know that vocabulary games can be an effective way for building students' word knowledge (Beck, McKeown, and Kucan 2002; Richek 2005). For example, Selvidge (2006) demonstrated improved content knowledge as well as subject area learning through the use of a board game focused on Egypt. Rubenstein and Thompson (2002) described how they adapted familiar games such as concentration, old maid, and go fish using elementary mathematical terminology (e.g., *square, foot, odd, cube, cent*) to increase their students' knowledge of content vocabulary.

From our experience, the key to using vocabulary games in the classroom lies in getting students to do the work—and getting each student to do a sufficient amount of work. When students write questions, for example, they have to consider the role that word meaning plays in the answers. Similarly, as they construct games, students have to consider the multiple meanings of words so that they don't confuse their players. There are a number of games that teachers can use to build students' vocabulary, including the following:

- *Crossword Puzzles*: Creating crossword puzzles requires students to focus on word meanings, providing just enough information but not too much information. Discovery Education offers a Web-based puzzle creation tool that students can use to create their masterpieces (http://puzzlemaker.school.discovery.com).

- Jeopardy! Wheel of Fortune, *and* Who Wants to Be a Millionaire: Following the format of popular TV quiz shows, students create questions and answers based on specific vocabulary words. Again, the goal is to provide increasingly difficult questions to elicit responses. There are free PowerPoint downloads students can use to create these games at http://jc-schools.net/tutorials/vocab/ppt-vocab.html.

- *Wordo*: Students enter vocabulary words into the squares of a bingo card and then write definitions for each of the terms (Cunningham 2000). The teacher can call definitions while students mark off the words. Again, the key is to have students develop the game. A sample Wordo card can be found in Figure 4.11.

- *Flip-a-Chip*: Lee Mountain (2002) developed this game that uses poker chips or any other small round chips. After being introduced to the game, students write prefixes, suffixes, and bases on the chips. They then flip the chips and determine if the resulting word is real or not. Mountain introduces the game with two chips. On the first, one side says *pro-* and the other says *re-*. On the second chip, one side says *-duce* and the other says *-voke*. By flipping the two chips, students see that they can make the following words: *produce*, *provoke*, *reduce*, and *revoke*. By adding affixes and roots themselves, students learn a variety of combinations that do and do not produce real words.

Of course there are many other vocabulary games that students can play to build their vocabulary. As you can see, each of these games involves students writing and using the words. Of course, they are also talking with one another and creating visuals. In doing so, they build their store of words and begin to use these words as they complete tasks, engage with others, and read increasingly complex texts.

■ The Takeaway

Vocabulary learners need time to build their understanding of words and terms through peer interactions. Regular use of partner and small-group

WORDO

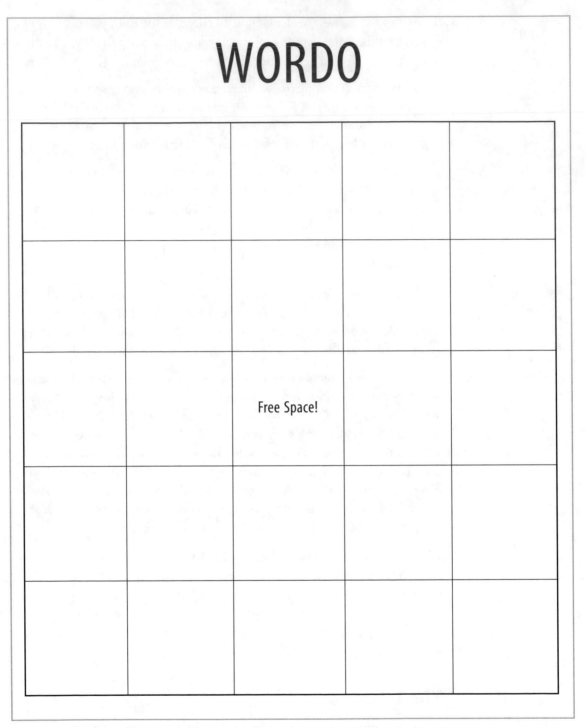

Free Space!

Figure 4.11 *Sample Wordo card*

discussion provides students with opportunities to clarify their thinking and extend each other's knowledge. Other interactions that utilize oral language include jigsaws, which encourage learners to retell new information, and reciprocal teaching, which formalizes the comprehension strategies used by proficient readers. Student think-alouds extend the work of the teacher, as described in Chapter 3, by shifting the cognitive load to the learner as he builds metacognition.

Other strategies capitalize on the visual arrangement of information in order for students to create knowledge maps that show relationships between and among words. Word mapping allows students to arrange information in a hierarchical manner, from larger concepts to smaller details. Semantic feature analysis adds another level of complexity, as students juxtapose ideas across two planes in a matrix form. Concept circles allow students to consider the attributes of a word, while a shades-of-meaning activity encourages students to see a group of related words on a continuum or gradient of intensity.

The final group of peer interaction activities ask learners to apply their growing word knowledge using writing. Working together, they analyze a list of words and link them into a paragraph that might predict the reading to come. Collaborative posters move small-group work from the task of one recorder to a shared responsibility where all members are required to contribute their ideas in writing. Lastly, students play and create original games for others utilizing the vocabulary of the content. These game development tasks extend student learning beyond passive experiences. Building vocabulary requires active learning, and peer interactions let students see words from the inside and outside—and help make word learning a part of *their* everyday discourse. Thus, the acquisition of words and ideas becomes central to their lives rather than something school focuscd, and wc all gct that much closer to achieving true content knowledge.

CHAPTER

5

Make It Personal

Consolidating Students' Word Learning
Through Individual Activities

IT MAY SOUND MELODRAMATIC, but spending just three minutes talking with a student about her work can be transformative for both the teacher and the learner. When we take the time to meet individually with students and invite them to articulate their reasoning about their independent work, it helps them consolidate their thinking and helps us identify strengths and needs with maximum efficiency. Why, then, has independent learning gotten a bad reputation over the years? In a word, *worksheets*. When you hear "independent work," the first image that comes to mind is one of students doing lots of fairly superficial worksheets in and out of school. We're not fans of endless streams of worksheets, either, and we are quite concerned at the amount of time students spend working independently. A large-scale study of 737 fifth-grade classrooms in thirty-three states found that students spent 38 percent of their time doing individual seatwork (Pianta et al. 2007).

As a profession, we've got to stop equating independent learning with busywork and instead give it the exalted place it deserves. Independent work should be a vital part of content area learning in general and vocabulary learning in particular. Think about it: without it, all our teaching disappears like wisps of smoke. It's in an individual student's solo work that we see she *has* learned—she has *applied* what we've taught her. Independent work is the final phase of the gradual release of responsibility model of instruction, capping off the modeling and guided practice phases of this model. Race (1996) argues that all learning is ultimately independent, in the sense that it doesn't really become known until it becomes a part of the individual's knowledge base—collective knowledge alone won't cut it. Our goal as teachers is for students to become independent learners. But this is where we think independent learning breaks down in too many classrooms: independent *for* whom and independent *from* whom? We need to consider whether an activity is contributing to students' knowledge of themselves as learners or if it is merely an assignment that keeps them independent from *us*.

What does an independent learner look like? Before we develop activities that we think will foster independence and further students' understandings, we've found it helpful to sketch a profile of such learners' features. Murdoch and Wilson (2006) analyzed the research on effective independent learners and synthesized the findings in three main characteristics:

- *Independent learners are self-motivators.* These students can establish goals and monitor their progress toward them, they are willing to take risks, and they welcome challenge.

- *Independent learners are self-managers.* They try to solve their own problems, manage their time, and think creatively.

- *Independent learners are self-appraisers.* They accurately assess what they know and don't know, they notice their own learning, and they act upon their learning by applying strategies they know to be useful for learning.

As you plan independent vocabulary activities, measure them against these qualities as a way to check their effectiveness. Ask yourself: "Does this activity significantly contribute to my students' development as self-motivated, self-managed, and self-appraising learners?" If we can be honest with ourselves about our independent learning practices, we will be in good stead.

> **Focus on Struggling Readers**
>
> Goal setting is important for all learners, but especially for students who are performing below grade-level expectations. As with other aspects of instruction, independent work should be differentiated. Confer with these students to discuss intermediate goals that are likely to result in success. Learners who can gauge their own progress as a series of achieved steps become more confident and motivated. Nothing breeds success like success.

■ Characteristics of Effective Individual Learning

What can't be lost in the discussion of independent learning (which needs to be part of the instructional design of a class) is the individual learner. The room may be bulging at the seams with twenty to thirty-five learners, but each is unique in terms of background knowledge, habits of mind, and interests. There isn't any practical way to teach each student individually, and even if there were, we wouldn't advocate for it anyway. But even in a crowd, we have to set the conditions for independent learning. The conditions for successful individual learning include the following:

- *Choice*: Learners need to see options in how they approach a task. That's why worksheets and end-of-chapter questions are so demoralizing. Activities that result in unique responses are more engaging.

- *Differentiation*: Differentiating instruction doesn't mean creating thirty-five different assignments, but it does mean varying tasks depending on the needs and proclivities of the student. This is especially true with vocabulary knowledge. Students don't arrive at our classroom door in possession of the same bank of words at their disposal. The vocabulary they are responsible for at the individual level should differ so that it aligns more closely with what they currently need to learn.

- *Relevance*: If it feels like busywork, it is doomed to fail. Teachers have to make sure students see how the individual activities relate to the unit of study. In addition, teachers should be explicit about the ways in which they are helping students develop into self-regulated learners.

■ Moving from Building to Consolidating

In the last chapter, we spoke of the need for students to build their knowledge of words through peer interactions. These collaborative experiences encourage learners to use specialized and technical vocabulary in their oral language, to negotiate meaning through joint development of knowledge maps, and to apply terminology during group writing. These building experiences must be followed by well-crafted individual activities that allow students to consolidate their understanding of the definitional, contextual, and conceptual knowledge of words.

Nagy (1988) reminds us that there are three conditions needed for a student to learn vocabulary: integration, repetition, and meaningful use. Individual learning experiences provide students with these opportunities in the following ways:

- *integration* with schemata through a focus on "sets of relationships," not isolated facts (10);

- *repetition* through multiple opportunities to encounter a new word in speech, reading, and writing; and

- *meaningful* use that "makes students think about the meaning of the word and demands they do some . . . processing of the word" (24).

The individual learning activities in this chapter were selected based on their properties of integration, repetition, and meaningful use. In addition, we looked for activities that met the needs of individual learners regarding choice, differentiation, and relevance. Finally, we analyzed each to determine whether the activity fostered development of students as self-motivators, self-managers, and self-appraisers. We have grouped these activities into three categories. The first group of activities asks students to log their knowledge in ways that cause them to consider what they know and don't know.

Creating a word card

The second category invites students to mentally and physically manipulate words using sorts, word cards, and mnemonic devices. The final type encourages them to compose using the targeted vocabulary.

Tracking, Reflecting, Knowing: Logs and Other Documents

The ability to know what one knows, as well as what is not known, is a key aspect to metacognitive awareness. The goal of this process isn't merely to catalog one's knowledge, but to set goals, a fundamental characteristic of a self-regulated learner (Ridley et al. 1992). The following activities encourage individual learners to notice their learning and witness their progress toward learning goals.

Vocabulary Self-Awareness— Self-Monitoring in Action

One of the reasons that vocabulary instruction has been so difficult to change revolves around the fact that students differ in their baseline understanding of words. Take, for example, a typical class of fourth-grade students. The differences in vocabulary knowledge in this group are likely to range by about three years. Some students will have word knowledge profiles of students in first or second grade while others will possess extensive vocabularies that would earn them high school–level scores on vocabulary assessments.

Understanding that there are differences in individual vocabulary attainment is the primary reason that this system works. We know that students benefit from modeling and using words with their peers. But if subject matter vocabulary instruction ended there, students would not attain high levels of literacy achievement. As teachers, we simply must provide opportunities for students to consolidate their vocabulary knowledge.

One of the ways we do this is through vocabulary self-assessments (e.g., Goodwin 2001). As words are encountered, students can add them to their self-awareness chart and determine if they know the word, have just heard the word, or if the word is a new one. While some words, especially technical words, are provided to everyone in the class, other words are given only to specific students. As such, each student might have different words on his vocabulary self-awareness chart. Both teachers and students can determine which words to add to their charts. We know that self-selection of vocabulary enhances students' motivation and achievement in learning new words (Ruddell and Shearer 2002). In addition, when students can explain their rationale for adding words to their chart, they develop their metacognitive skills and word consciousness. Even further, as they incorporate definitions and examples into their knowledge base, they consolidate their knowledge of inside-the-word and outside-the-word problem-solving strategies.

We've modified a vocabulary self-assessment chart, which can be found in Figure 5.1. Students enter a date for the level of knowledge they have when they first encounter the word. As they become more comfortable with the word, they add dates in advancing levels. For example, third-grade student April was reading the book *The Paper Bag Princess* (Munsch 1992). As she incorporated specific terms into her knowledge base, you can see that she changed the dates. It's important to note that not all of the words on April's chart could be found on the charts of her peers. These are the words that April and her teacher thought were important for her to learn.

A–Z Charts— Topical Words Lists

A–Z charts are another way that individuals can track what they know and what they learn, in terms of subject area vocabulary, during a unit of study. These simple charts, like the one in Figure 5.2, contain alphabetically arranged blocks for students to record the words they know based on the given topic. There are a number of ways to use an A–Z chart (Allen 2000). We prefer to ask students to identify words and phrases they know about the topic and log them on the chart as an anticipatory activity, before any

Word	???	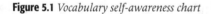	☺	Sentence	Definition
ashes	11/6		11/10	Everything the dragon breathed turned in to ashes	The stuff that's left from burning
breathed		11/7	11/10	The air was hot that Elizabeth breathed	When someone takes a breath and lets it out
expensive		11/8	11/10	Prince Ronald's clothes were very expensive	costs a lot
fiery	11/7		11/14	The dragon had fiery breath that burned up the tree	Burning up with fire

??? = a word that is new to me
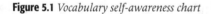 = I have heard this word before
☺ = I know the definition and I can use it in a sentence

Figure 5.1 *Vocabulary self-awareness chart*

instruction. Then, as the unit progresses, individual students add words to their individual charts.

As part of her social studies unit on the U.S. government, Ms. Medina distributed blank copies of an A–Z chart to her students. She asked them to identify words and phrases that they knew related to the California third-grade standard of recognizing "national landmarks, symbols, and essential documents that create a sense of community among citizens and exemplify cherished ideals" (www.cde.ca.gov/be/st/ss/documents/histsocscistnd.pdf). Given that this was the first time she had used an A–Z chart, students were unsure what to do. Kari was concerned and asked, "Is this something that we can get a bad grade on?" Ms. Medina assured her students that this was not a test, but rather an opportunity to identify what they already knew so that she could focus her instruction on what each student needed to know.

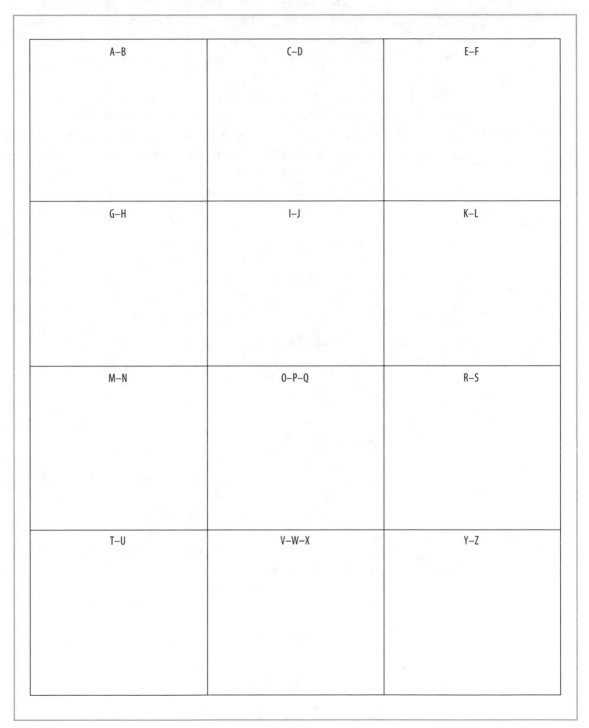

A–B	C–D	E–F
G–H	I–J	K–L
M–N	O–P–Q	R–S
T–U	V–W–X	Y–Z

Figure 5.2 *A–Z chart*

The students started working, listing words and phrases that they associated with national symbols. "Remember that you don't need to think of them in alphabetical order," Ms. Medina told them. "If the first word you think of starts with an *m*, write it down!"

As students finished this opening exercise, Ms. Medina asked them to draw a line in each box under the last word or phrase entered. Over the course of two weeks, as students engaged in the unit of study, Ms. Medina reminded them to update their A–Z charts. They added information from class discussions, readings, and films to their charts. Kari's chart, with a dashed line drawn under each word that she knew at the outset of the unit, is shown in Figure 5.3. Note how many more words she knew by the end of

A-B	C-D	E-F
Bald Eagle Bell AMERICA the Beautiful	Dollar Capitol building Declaration of Independence	Flag
G-H	**I-J**	**K-L**
	Jefferson Monument	Lincoln Memorial Liberty Bell
M-N	**O-P-Q**	**R-S**
Mount Rushmore National Anthem	Pledge of Allegiance	Statue of Liberty
T-U	**V-W-X**	**Y-Z**
Towers that fell down	White House Washington Monument World trade center Vietnam Memorial	

Figure 5.3 *Kari's A–Z chart on national symbols*

the unit. There are some boxes with no lines because she did not have any words to include during the opening activity.

Importantly, A–Z charts also help teachers identify words that students believe they know. This information can be used as a formative assessment in that the teacher may notice that some students don't know a lot of words related to the content being studied and, thus, need additional instruction. The teacher may also notice that some students are not adding to their A–Z charts and wonder if this group of students is failing to focus on word learning. In addition, teachers can use A–Z charts as a source of checking vocabulary knowledge. By sitting with a student and looking at her chart, the teacher can discuss word meanings and see if the student really has a grasp of the words listed on the chart.

Vocabulary Journals— Keeping Track of Words

As we have discussed, students learn and retain vocabulary in a variety of ways. Of course, students need opportunities to interact with the words, especially in peer contexts. However, students also need a place to keep track of the words they're learning. An effective way to accomplish this is through a vocabulary journal (Frey and Fisher 2007). Students clarify unfamiliar words or phrases by listing them on a chart in their vocabulary journal. They can identify words themselves or their teachers can identify words to be added to the journal.

Vocabulary journal entries can have all kinds of components. Of course, there are no hard-and-fast rules about what to include in a vocabulary journal. In our own teaching, we focus students on specialized vocabulary words. As can be seen in the vocabulary journal in Figure 5.4, students were asked to collect words that had meanings different from what they thought. This assignment also required that students think about how they figured out a word—from context clues, word parts, or resources.

Consolidating Understandings: Word-Manipulation Activities

The physical and mental manipulation of words is an extension of the visual methods outlined in the previous chapter. These techniques cause learners to consolidate definitional, contextual, and conceptual understandings of words in completing sorting activities, creating word cards for studying, and developing mnemonic devices for promoting recall and retrieval.

Word Sorts— Organizing Word Knowledge

Sorting words causes students to consider the relationships between and among groups of words. At its simplest level, this activity involves a student in grouping related words into categories by considering the attributes or properties represented by each word.

WORD	WHAT I THINK IT MEANS	WHAT IT ACTUALLY MEANS	CLUES (context or parts)	WHERE I FOUND OUT

Figure 5.4 *Vocabulary journal*

There are three basic kinds of word sorts: closed, open, and conceptual. Closed sorts come with categories furnished in advance by the teacher, while open sorts require the student to develop original categories (Bear et al. 2007). Word sorts for younger learners involve phonics and spelling patterns, while the ones we use with older elementary students are often conceptual. These sorts should be performed using words printed on individual slips of paper. While this may seem burdensome to prepare, the usefulness of a sorting activity is in providing the maximum amount of flexibility to the learner as he contemplates possible categorical arrangements. We have tried to take the easy way out and given students a list of words for them to write and have discovered that they are far less likely to experiment. They dislike erasing anything once they've written it and will sort using the most obvious categories possible. In order to reduce your preparation time, ask students to cut their own word slips and write the assigned words on each. They can glue the words onto a notebook page and write an explanation of their thinking.

As an example, Figure 5.5 contains a word sort that Josiah did with onset and rime patterns. As a first grader, he's learning to categorize words by their ending spelling patterns. Figure 5.6 contains Madison's word sort for words related to the sky. Her fifth-grade class has been working with these ideas for several weeks and Madison has a good sense of how these vocabulary words fit together.

"When I spoke to Madison about her word sort, I realized that this was a student who was moving beyond basic understanding and seeing the relationship between the words," said her teacher Ms. Buehner. "She can talk

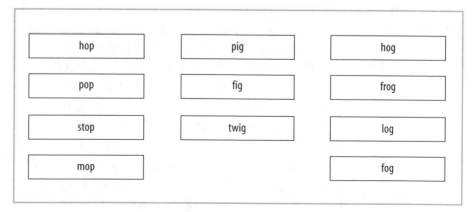

Figure 5.5 *Josiah's open word sort*

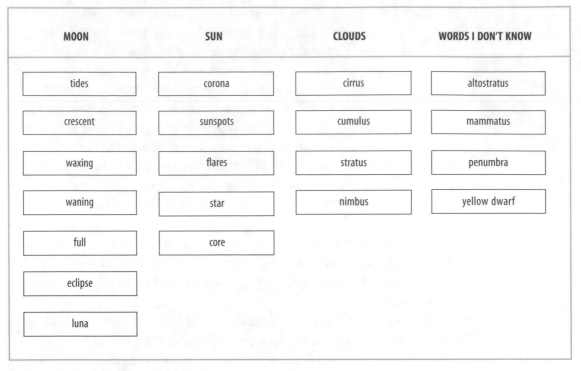

MOON	SUN	CLOUDS	WORDS I DON'T KNOW
tides	corona	cirrus	altostratus
crescent	sunspots	cumulus	mammatus
waxing	flares	stratus	penumbra
waning	star	nimbus	yellow dwarf
full	core		
eclipse			
luna			

Figure 5.6 *Madison's open sort of sky-related terms*

about each of these terms and knows which are observable and which are not. She is displaying reasoning that other students don't yet have. This tells me that she is ready to be challenged even further."

Word Cards—Consolidating Through Repeated Practice

Word cards are a powerful way for students to think about words, especially because they can be used to help students consolidate their understanding of vocabulary terms. Of course, word selection is critical. Students should be spending time focused on words that they need to know, either from their own selection or based on terms their teachers suggest.

One of the ways that students consolidate their understanding of vocabulary is to focus on the terms longer than a few seconds. That's one of the reasons that word cards are effective: they take a little time and effort to complete. In addition, word cards provide students an opportunity to review key terms. That's the other reason that they're effective: learners need multiple opportunities to interact with words in order to truly know them.

Our vocabulary cards are based on the Frayer model (e.g., Frayer, Frederick, and Klausmeier 1969) and encourage learners to think about new vocabulary through definition, contrasts, and visual representations (see Figure 5.7). They are typically developed using five-by-seven-inch index cards divided into four quadrants. Naturally, there are a number of variations of word cards. Some teachers like sentences written on the cards; others do not. Some teachers focus on synonyms and antonyms, while others do not. We prefer to have students illustrate the term on the word card as this requires them to think about the word using a different part of their brain. Phillip's word card for the word *latitude* from a fourth-grade investigation of physical geography can be found in Figure 5.8.

Mnemonics—
Memory
Builders

Keyword mnemonics were first used to teach students studying a foreign language (Raugh and Atkinson 1975) and soon became popular for teaching vocabulary for any learner (Pressley, Levin, and Delaney 1983). The word *mnemonics* comes from the Greek word *mnemonikos*, meaning mindful. Mnemonic devices are used to recall information. For example, many of us have learned to use FOIL to remind ourselves of the steps for multiplying binomials—*first, outside, inside, last*. Doug memorized the lobes of the brain for his neuroanatomy class using FPOT: *frontal, parietal, occipital*, and *temporal*. This is called a peg mnemonic because each letter reminds us of an item on a list.

The keyword method of vocabulary attainment involves two other aspects of mnemonic devices: an acoustical element and a visual one. It is believed that memory is enhanced when two stimuli are closely associated with one another, known more formally as dual coding theory (Paivio 1969). These techniques are widely used for memorization and recall of complex information in the fields of pathology, medicine, pharmacology, and aviation. For example, a mnemonic that uses dual coding involves

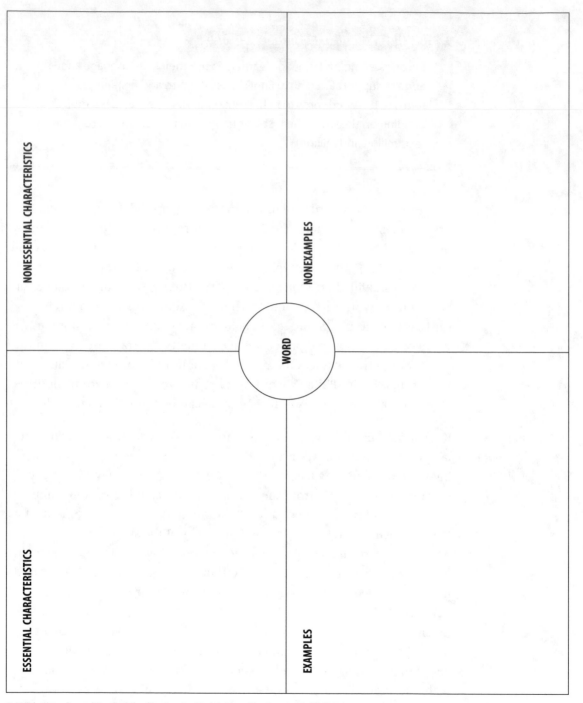

NONESSENTIAL CHARACTERISTICS

NONEXAMPLES

WORD

ESSENTIAL CHARACTERISTICS

EXAMPLES

Figure 5.7 *Vocabulary card based on Frayer model*

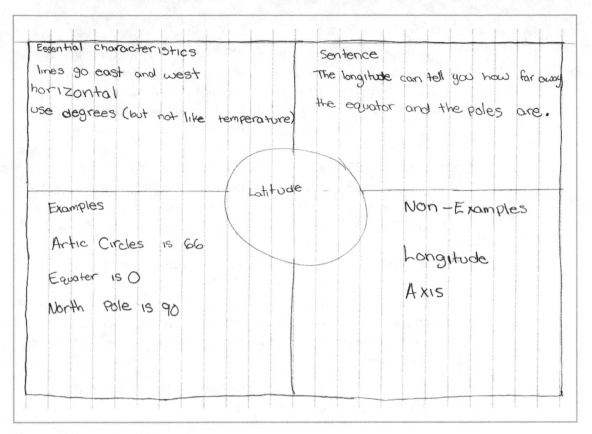

Figure 5.8 *Philip's word card for* latitude

Felty's syndrome, a complication that can arise because of rheumatoid arthritis. One of the markers of the disease is that the spleen can be *felt* (Felty's) upon examination. Many people who have passed national professional board examinations owe their thanks in part to mnemonics for recalling information.

Let's return to the word *mnemonic* to demonstrate the usefulness of keyword learning as it relates to roots and word derivation. We told you that it stems from the Greek word for mindfulness. The word is also closely related to Mnemosyne, the mother of the Muses in mythology. Now add a visual to that—imagine a Greek goddess who *mindfully* watches over her daughters. She encourages them to *remember* where they came from, and to keep the *memory* of their family close to their hearts. That mental image of the mindful mother along with the acoustically similar words *mindful, remember,* and *memory* consolidate a dual association in your mind. Chances are that if you have invested your attention in that word, you will recall the word and its image long after you close this book.

Mnemonics are a useful way for individual learners to mentally manipulate sound and image to create a memory that can be retrieved on demand. We teach our students to use mnemonics as a way to independently learn information and vocabulary. In fact, the information we shared about Mnemosyne is how we introduce the technique to our students. We ask them to think of peg mnemonics they have already learned, and we usually hear about HOMES to recall the names of the Great Lakes (Huron, Ontario, Michigan, Erie, and Superior), or Please Excuse My Dear Aunt Sally to remind them of the order of operations in mathematics (parentheses, exponents, multiplication, division, addition, subtraction). We also give them opportunities to develop their own peg and keyword mnemonics, as the most valuable ones seem to be those that are created by the learner rather than provided by the teacher.

For example, Kevin had been trying to figure out a way to remember the thirteen colonies. Kevin had used mnemonics with some success, so he decided to check the Internet to see what he could find. The one he found that humored him was

Good (Georgia) Students (South Carolina) Need (North Carolina) Very (Virginia) Many (Maryland) Dogs (Delaware)
   Never (New Jersey) Pet (Pennsylvania) New (New York) Cats (Connecticut)
   Roaring (Rhode Island) Mad (Massachusetts) New Hamsters (New Hampshire)

He liked this idea and wanted to make his own, so he listed the letters of the colonies: G, S, N, V, M, D, N, P, N, C, R, M, N. Not finding any obvious words, he began to create sentences. He crossed off letters as he used them, knowing that he did not need to memorize the colonies in any particular order. In the course of a few minutes, he created something he found satisfactory:

Grandma screamed no more dogs. Victor needs peace not crazy running mutts now.

He sketched a cartoon drawing of an older woman shouting at a bunch of dogs with an older man trying to sleep in a hammock. "I imaged my gramma yelling at the dogs while Grandpa Victor tried to sleep." Of course, each of these colonies represents far more information than the label alone implies. But Kevin's creation of a personal mnemonic allowed him to recall a sequence of information and access the schema he had developed for this content and words used to convey the information.

To Write Is to Know: Composing Activities

In addition to logging words and physically and mentally manipulating words, students consolidate their understanding when they compose using subject area vocabulary. Composing with scaffolds and supports compels learners to focus on word meanings and how words fit into sentences and paragraphs. It is important to note that asking students to write using targeted vocabulary comes later in the process of developing academic word knowledge. Students working at the individual learning level have had multiple exposures to words in order to develop some depth and breadth to their word knowledge.

Generative Sentences— Constructing from the Given

One of the ways students consolidate their knowledge of vocabulary is to use specific words in constructed sentences (Fisher and Frey 2007). Generative sentences involve students in constructing sentences from words that are given to them. Fearn and Farnan call this practice a "given word sentence" (2001, 87). We have extended their ideas and focus on the generative nature of the composing process that requires students to move from the word, to the sentence, to the paragraph level.

This instructional routine allows students to expand their sentences and to be able to use the word choices and mechanics that are necessary in order to convey information. Essentially, the teacher identifies a letter or word and the place in a sentence where the word will be used. Students then write sentences with the given components. The key to generative sentences is to vary the placement of the word (e.g., first position, last position, some numbered position) and the length of the sentence (e.g., exactly *x* number of words, fewer than *x* number of words, or more than *x* number of words). These variations require that students consider the complexity of the word and how it can be used, correctly, in a sentence.

For example, in our study of a gradual release of responsibility for writing instruction (Fisher and Frey 2003), we asked struggling readers to write the letter *v* on their paper. The next instruction was to write a word with the letter *v* in the third position. We then recorded a list of words on the dry-erase board. Students were able to see the variation of words that share this characteristic, such as *love, have, give, dove,* and *advice.* Following this, we asked students to use their word in a sentence. Here's a sample of the sentences they created:

> I love my family, especially James.
> The dove is a sign of peace.
> You best get some advice on that hairdo.

Once students are familiar with the task, the teacher can focus on specialized and vocabulary words. By requiring that specific words be placed in specific places within sentences, we ensure that students use their knowledge of vocabulary and grammar to demonstrate their thinking. We recommend that students complete five generative sentences per class per day. Teachers of primary students can adapt this to a shared writing activity. This provides them practice with composing using specific words. Our experience suggests that the selected words should be a mix of specialized and technical terms. Importantly, this individual activity provides the teacher with an opportunity to check for understanding. By reviewing students' generative sentences, the teacher can determine the depth of students' understanding and identify students who need additional assistance.

Take, for example, the following sentences written by two different students. The sentences clearly demonstrate the two students' thinking about the word *patriots*. The prompt required that students use the word *patriots* in the fourth position.

The world champion Patriots are the best team ever!
The very brave patriots in the American Revolution helped the colonists win.

Both students used the term correctly, one for a football team in New England and one for the heroes of the American Revolution. While their teacher was focused on colonial American history, one of these students was not.

While focused on animal adaptation, a teacher used generative sentences on a daily basis. During the part of the unit on physical adaptation, the teacher shared the book *Animal Disguises* (Weber 2004). Given that the words in the book should have been familiar to her students, this science teacher asked her students to compose the following five sentences:

1. *camouflage* in the first position of a sentence of any length

2. *disguise(s)* in the fourth position of a sentence of more than six words

3. *habitat* in the last position of a sentence of fewer than ten words

4. *features* in the third position of a sentence of any length

5. an *if . . . then* sentence about animal adaptation

It is clear from Huynh's writing (Figure 5.9) that he understands most of these words. Given his response to the prompt about *habitat*, and the lack of

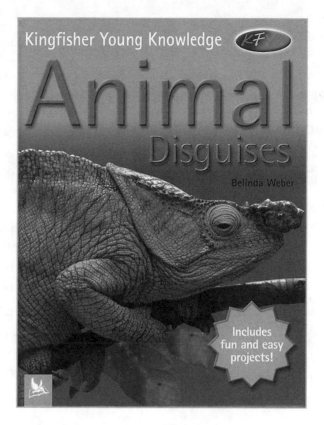

> 1. <u>Camouflage</u> is a way for animals to hide.
>
> 2. A moth, can <u>disguise</u> itself to hide from birds.
>
> 3. An animal's house is called his <u>habitat</u>.
>
> 4. An animal's <u>features</u> make it special.
>
> 5. If an animal can't hide, <u>then</u> it might get eaten.

Figure 5.9 *Huynh's generative sentences related to* Animal Disguises

sophistication this response demonstrates, his teacher decided to focus some additional instructional time with him related to the concept of habitats.

Writing Frames— Providing Structure for Words

We have noticed that the use of writing models such as sentence and paragraph frames provides students with scaffolds such that they can write more sophisticated compositions (Fisher and Frey 2007). These writing frames also help students focus on the words they are learning by removing some of the task demands related to composition. We know that students write less sophisticated sentences and paragraphs when they have not internalized academic writing.

College composition experts Gerald Graff and Cathy Birkenstein (2006) recommend the use of frames (they call them templates) as an effective way for developing students' academic writing skills. They suggest that students be systematically taught these frames, as they are models of academic writing. They defend the use of frames or templates by suggesting

> after all, even the most creative forms of expression depend on established patterns and structures. Most songwriters, for instance, rely on a time-honored verse-chorus-verse pattern, and few people would call Shakespeare uncreative because he didn't invent the sonnet or dramatic forms that he used to such dazzling effect. . . . Ultimately, then, creativity and originality lie not in the avoidance of established forms, but in the imaginative use of them. (10–11)

As Graff and Birkenstein correctly note, writing frames help students incorporate established norms of academic writing. Writing frames provide students practice in the discourse patterns expected of educated citizens. In addition, based on our classroom experiences, we've found that writing frames provide students an opportunity to consolidate their understanding of specialized and technical terms as they use them to share their thinking.

At the most basic level, teachers can use frames around specific words to help students incorporate target words into their writing. Consider the use of writing frames related to persuasion. The students in Mr. McMurtry's class were focused on developing their persuasive writing skills. They did so by incorporating a number of frames into their habits. A number of sample frames related to persuasive writing can be found in Figure 5.10.

Importantly, writing frames are not limited to use in English language arts. They can be used when students are engaged in science and social studies as well. For example, during science, students were provided with a summary writing frame based on the work of Lewis and Wray (1995), which read:

Making a claim

- My own view is that _____, because _____.

- Though I agree that _____, I still maintain that _____.

- She argues _____, and I agree, because _____.

Supporting/critiquing a claim

- Her argument that _____ is supported by _____, _____, and _____.

- For example, _____ shows that _____.

- Their assertion that _____ is contradicted by _____, _____, and _____.

Introducing and addressing a counterargument

- Of course, some might disagree with my claim and say that _____.

- Some might object that _____, but I would reply that _____.

- While it is true that _____, that does not necessarily mean that _____.

Stating a conclusion or summing up an argument

- In conclusion, I believe _____.

- In sum: _____ is demonstrated by _____ and _____.

- For these reasons, _____ should be _____.

From *Learning Words Inside and Out*. Porstmouth, NH: Heinemann. © 2009 Glencoe Literature. Used with permission of Glencoe/McGraw-Hill.

Figure 5.10 *Persuasive writing frames*

> Although I already knew that _____, I have learned
> some new facts about _____. For example, I learned
> that _____. I also learned that _____.
> Another fact I learned is _____. However, the most
> interesting thing I learned was _____.

With repeated practice with writing frames, at both the sentence and paragraph levels, students become increasingly proficient in their writing and this writing is increasingly academic (Jones and Thomas 2006). To accomplish this, students must consolidate their understanding of new vocabulary. This individual task also allows teachers to determine their students' level of understanding of specific words and to make instructional decisions about which students need additional reteaching. A sample of student writing using the above writing frame can be found in Figure 5.11.

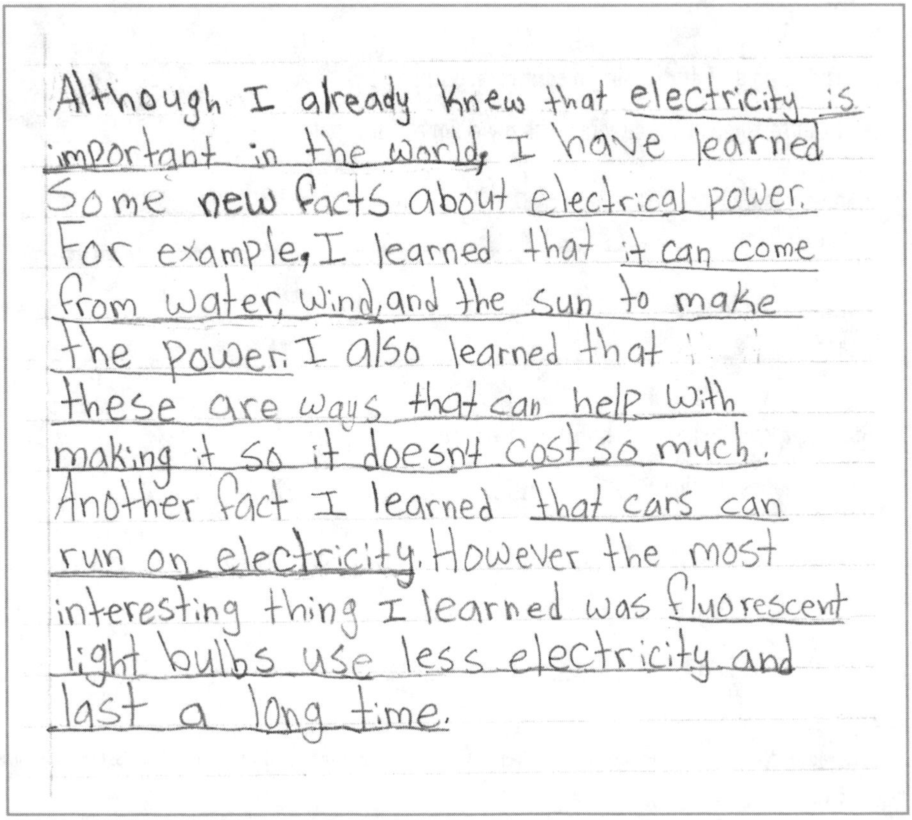

Although I already knew that electricity is important in the world, I have learned some new facts about electrical power. For example, I learned that it can come from water, wind, and the sun to make the power. I also learned that these are ways that can help with making it so it doesn't cost so much. Another fact I learned that cars can run on electricity. However the most interesting thing I learned was fluorescent light bulbs use less electricity and last a long time.

Figure 5.11 *Student writing using a frame*

■ Assessing Individual Learning of Vocabulary

We've left the topic of assessment until now because we believe that measurement practices encompass the word learning across teacher modeling, peer interaction, and individual learning. At each point along the way, there should be formative assessment practices that parallel instructional goals. We agree with Blachowicz and Fisher's (2002) reminder that the assessments used should measure both the depth and the breadth of students' word knowledge. Therefore, multiple-choice quizzes that ask students to supply a single definition are unlikely to meet the depth criteria of good vocabulary assessment. In the same regard, artificially isolating words and testing them as if they were unrelated to other words and ideas won't get us to a measure of breadth, either. We know the lure of Scantron sheets can tempt us all into evaluating our students' vocabulary knowledge in this way. But just because it yields a number that we can write into a grade book doesn't mean we have learned anything about what our students know.

Take a look at the assessment opportunities presented by the learning activities described in this book. To select an activity to use as an assessment, you first need to determine what you want to assess. Is it your students' existing knowledge? If so, a vocabulary self-awareness chart provides richer information than a multiple-choice test ever could. Do you want to look at vocabulary development over the course of a unit of study? Then an A–Z chart works well. To help you, we've listed dimensions of vocabulary assessment and corresponding activities from this book in Figure 5.12.

■ The Takeaway

A major goal of elementary education is to teach children the habits necessary for independent learning. However, what passes for independent learning in many classrooms has little to do with fostering independence. A necessary outcome of independent learning should be that the activity promotes learners' growth as self-motivators, self-managers, and self-appraisers. The needs of individual students must be considered as well, particularly when it comes to choice, differentiation, and relevance.

Students can develop their own metacognition through activities like vocabulary self-awareness charts, A–Z charts, and vocabulary journals. All of these encourage students to be word users and to notice how their own learning evolves over time. Individual learners also benefit from the physical and mental manipulation of words, as it allows them to develop

Dimension of Vocabulary Learning	Vocabulary Activity
Existing word knowledge	vocabulary self-awareness chart text impressions
Growth in vocabulary knowledge	A–Z chart vocabulary self-awareness chart
Application of vocabulary knowledge	generative sentences paragraph frames journals student think-alouds peer discussions
Word relationships (hierarchical and linear)	semantic feature analyses word maps shades of meaning word sorts
Knowledge of attributes	concept circles word maps word cards word sorts
Metacognitive awareness	vocabulary self-awareness chart student think-alouds mnemonics word cards word sorts

Figure 5.12 *Turning vocabulary learning into vocabulary assessment*

extensive knowledge maps. Techniques such as word sorts and word cards draw their attention to the relationships between and among words. Keyword and peg mnemonics equip students with distinct study skills that help them master large amounts of information. In addition, composition activities like generative sentences and paragraph frames let learners experiment with words in context. Writing activities like this are not used at the beginning of word instruction; rather, they come after the learner has had opportunities to develop breadth and depth of vocabulary knowledge.

CHAPTER

6

Make It a Priority

▪ Creating a Schoolwide Focus on Learning Words

A FOURTH GRADER NAMED SABRINA recently stopped Nancy in the hallway to ask about a muse. Having known Nancy for a few years, Sabrina knew that Nancy was not only interested in the arts but had all kinds of trivia in her brain. Sabrina wanted to read more about muses and hoped to find her own muse. Nancy didn't know why Sabrina was suddenly interested in the idea of a muse. She wondered what had sparked this new interest. "The word *museum* is one of this week's words," Sabrina explained, "and my teacher talked about words with *muse* in them, like *amuse*, *amusement*, *music*, and *bemused*."

Nancy talked about the original nine Greek Muses and how they were thought to inspire artists. "But," Nancy added, "a muse can be anywhere or anything. It doesn't have to be a person. You might amuse yourself and find your muse in a book or while you're walking home."

At Sabrina's school, the entire faculty and student body learn five words each week. In this chance encounter in the hallway, Nancy furthered Sabrina's understanding of one of the words. Pleased with this new interest, Nancy dashed down to the library later that day and with the help of the librarian found *You Can't Take a Balloon into the Metropolitan Museum*, by Jacqueline Preiss Weitzman and Robin Preiss Glasser (1999), and checked it out for Sabrina.

"Hi, Sabrina," Nancy said, catching her as she headed down the hallway for the bus. "Look what I found in the library. If you want to read more about museums and muses for amusement, this looks good."

"Sure," Sabrina said with a smile and opened the book, reading it on the way to the bus.

This story sounds like one of those too-good-to-be true scenes in a Hallmark Hall of Fame movie, but this kind of thing occurs often when schools sustain a schoolwide initiative. Five words of the week and wide reading efforts, where students read books of their choice often based on recommendations from teachers, extend students' thinking, vocabulary, and background knowledge. Look at what these two initiatives do for vocabulary learning in this school. They make word learning inescapable for kids, but in a way that has a sportlike, team-building spirit.

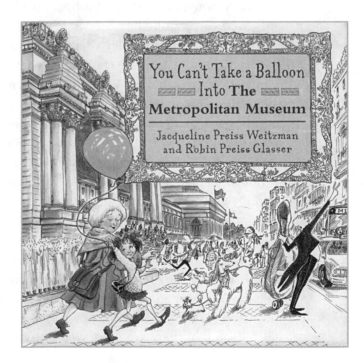

Words get a workout all week; teachers make an effort to work them into the day-to-day conversation, and in so doing, they send kids the message that vocabulary isn't the stuff of SAT prep, but the currency of talk, of socializing with peers, *and* of academic achievement.

As has been documented numerous times, schools with a clear focus outperform schools that lack a focus. For example, Reeves (2000) reported that establishing a schoolwide instructional focus was one of the most important actions that a school could take to improve performance. Similarly, in a study of schools that "beat the odds," Langer (2001) reported that schoolwide attention to literacy was one of the indicators of successful performance. Similarly, our work with a large urban elementary school yielded steady gains in literacy achievement (Fisher and Frey 2007). Given the importance of vocabulary, both for reading and writing, it seems reasonable to suggest vocabulary development should become a schoolwide endeavor rather than be left up to the discretion of individual teachers. Two schoolwide vocabulary efforts our research has shown to be effective are words of the week and wide reading.

■ Words of the Week

As we have noted throughout this book, students need to know a lot of words to be successful. They need to learn more than the words that are found in the current texts they're reading. We take exception with the idea that all of the words selected for instruction should come from texts students are expect to read. While this view may be controversial in some circles, especially those who suggest that "we teach words only in context," our experience indicates that sometimes students need to learn words that they will be able to use to figure out other words while reading. Of course, most of the words we teach are taught in context. Our out-of-context vocabulary work is known as the Words of the Week, or WOW, initiative.

In the primary grades, kindergarten through second, the words of the week are the Dolch sight words (e.g., www.dolchsightwords.org, see Appendix). Teachers organize these into groupings of three to five terms. For example, a first-grade teacher focused on pronouns one week: *his*, *her*, *him*, and *them*. Another teacher organized them alphabetically and taught *take*, *thank*, *them*, *then*, and *think* during another week. Given that there are more weeks than words on the Dolch list, teachers often add high-frequency prefix and suffix words to the lists and use onset and rime spelling patterns appropriate for the grade level on alternating weeks.

In the upper grades, the words of the week have a common prefix, suffix, root, or base. The primary goal is to provide students instruction in using these word parts to make educated guesses about unfamiliar words as they are reading. Engaging in a words of the week initiative schoolwide gives teachers an opportunity to provide instruction relevant to their content area related to the words. When done schoolwide, all students learn the words, talk about the words, and are expected to add the words to their oral language and written vocabularies.

Josephine is an English language learner who speaks a number of languages, but her knowledge of English was limited when she arrived at her American school in the fourth grade. Consider Josephine's increased knowledge about words following a week focused on five words containing the prefix *mal-*, meaning bad. The five example words were *malice*, *malign*, *malodorous*, *malnourished*, and *malady*. Even if Josephine didn't master all five of these words, she is likely to remember that *mal-* is bad and make an educated guess about meaning when she comes into contact with the words *malcontent* and *maladjusted*.

There is evidence that focusing on affixes and bases is helpful for students. For example, Baumann, Font, Edwards, and Boland (2005) examined the effectiveness of teaching word-part and context clues to promote word knowledge. According to their data, students must learn to use strategies and skills such as solving unknown words by understanding how affixes affect root word meaning. In their discussion about the myths and realities of teaching reading, Adams and Henry (1997) noted that attention to affixes was critical, especially after students had mastered early phonics. Without an increasingly sophisticated understanding of the ways words work, students fail to advance in their literacy skills.

If you doubt this at all, ask an informed and financially secure parent if he or she paid for an SAT prep course for his or her high school–aged child. In that course, the student likely received more instruction on affixes than during all of the combined time affixes were taught in school. Understanding affixes and roots or bases helps us think about words. Yes, many teenagers forget what they learned in the SAT crash course. But imagine if this information were part of the regular school day, year after year. We just don't think that parents should have to pay for this instruction when we could infuse it into the school day.

The best implementation of WOW comes when an entire grade level agrees to focus on five related words every week. Of course, an individual teacher can also implement a WOW initiative. When the entire school participates, the word lists can be generated well in advance of the school year. In some schools, a WOW committee identifies specific prefixes, suffixes, roots, and bases and sends this list to all teachers. Teachers then nominate words for inclusion on the list. The committee can then select the five best examples for use during each week of the school year. An example of one school's effort can be found in Figure 6.1.

Teachers formally introduce the words using instructional strategies that initiate students to definitional meaning and encourage multiple exposures. One of the ways to increase attention to these words is to print them on card stock for each participating teacher so that teachers can create a word wall of these words. Some teachers add each of the five words each week to their word wall and create a semester-long list, while others have only the five current words up each week. Of course, word walls aren't limited to high-frequency prefix, suffix, and root words. Many of the teachers with whom we work include content words in their word walls.

Using Word Walls in Content Area Classrooms

Word walls are an organized collection of words displayed in large letters on a wall. Simple enough. But students don't learn words from word walls by osmosis; simply being in the presence of words does not help students learn them. Word walls, to be effective, must be used. For example, teachers can review meanings of the word wall words, talking with students about definitions, additional examples, and related words. Students can write creative and interesting sentences using their word wall words. Of course, they should be asked to write sentences only after they have some familiarity with the words. Word walls help

	week 2	Week 3	Week 4
prefix: -re (to do again)	root: port (to carry)	prefix: un- (not)	suffix: -ion (act of)
react	airport	undo	adoption
reread	seaport	unfair	exception
reuse	transport	unclear	digestion
rename	support	uninteresting	action
retell	export	unlikely	admission

Week 5	Week 6	Week 7	Week 8
prefix: -de (opposite)	root: auto (self)	prefix: mis- (wrong)	root: graph (writing or drawing)
defrost	automobile	misfit	autograph
decease	automatic	misspoke	graphic
deceive	autobiography	misbehave	geography
decide	autograph	misfortune	photograph
declare	automate	misfeed	biography

Week 9	Week 10	Week 11	Week 12
suffix: -ness (state or condition)	prefix: mal- (bad)	root: muse (to gaze or be astonished)	suffix: -able (able to)
haplessness	malice	museum	capable
wildness	malign	amuse	variable
lowliness	malodorous	amusement	closeable
bitterness	malady	unamused	collectable
selflessness	malnourished	bemused	lovable

Figure 6.1 *One school's WOW affixes, root, and word choices, grades 3–6*

Word wall

students remember words because of the frequency with which they can interact with the words. Most importantly, word wall interactions should be fun. Students can guess words based on information that the teacher provides. Alternatively, students can create bingo cards with the words and the teacher can call definitions until someone gets bingo. We ask students to create vocabulary word cards for each of the words on the wall.

Another version of a vocabulary card based on the Frayer model discussed in Chapter 5 (Frayer, Frederick, and Klausmeier 1969) was developed by Audra, a first-grade math student (see Figure 6.2). This particular card contains the word in the upper left quadrant, what the word means in the student's own words in the upper right quadrant, what the word doesn't mean or an antonym in the lower right quadrant, and an illustration of the word in the lower left quadrant. Typically, these cards have a hole punched in one corner and are maintained on a ring. We ask students to have five adults (family, community members, and teachers) sign the back of a card following a conversation about what the word means. Not only does this increase the number of times the student interacts with the card, but it also provides students an authentic opportunity to use the word while speaking.

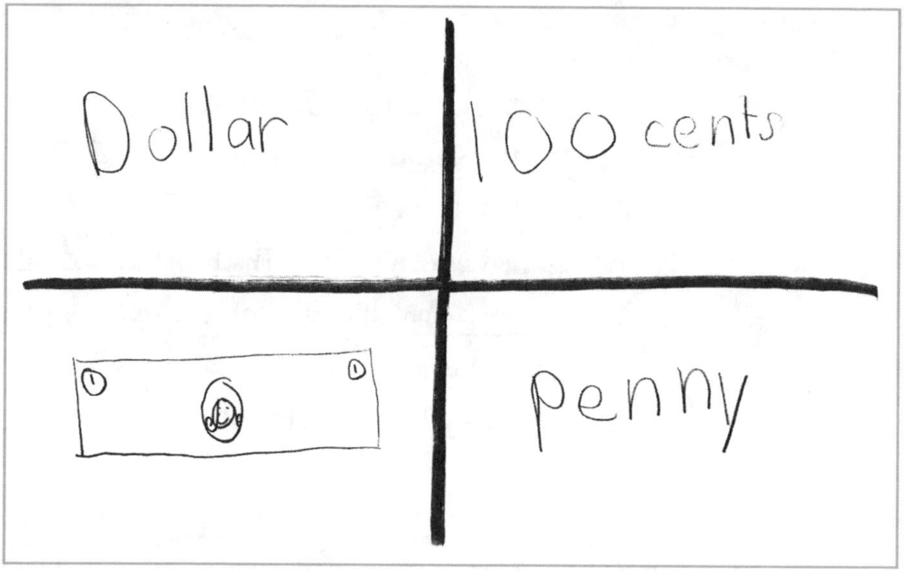

Figure 6.2 *Audra's word card for* dollar

Over time, and with practice, students begin to incorporate words of the week into their oral and written vocabularies. For example, Steve expressed his opinion about a book he had just finished reading with the comment "I had to *reread* it because it was *extraordinary*!" Another student was quoted as reporting, "I'm turning in an *abbreviated* homework." Words of the week also appear in student writing. Figure 6.3 contains a paragraph on the Pony Express from Tricia, a fourth-grade social studies student. We've underlined the words that were previously taught as words of the week.

■ Building Word Knowledge Through Wide Reading

How often have you met an articulate person and thought, *That's someone who's well read*? The product of a person's reading habits are evidenced in her communications. It comes as no surprise to teachers that students who read more also possess a richer oral and written vocabulary (Stanovich and Cunningham 1992). Repeated exposure to the printed word results in a growing mental vocabulary bank in much the same way that exercise improves muscle memory.

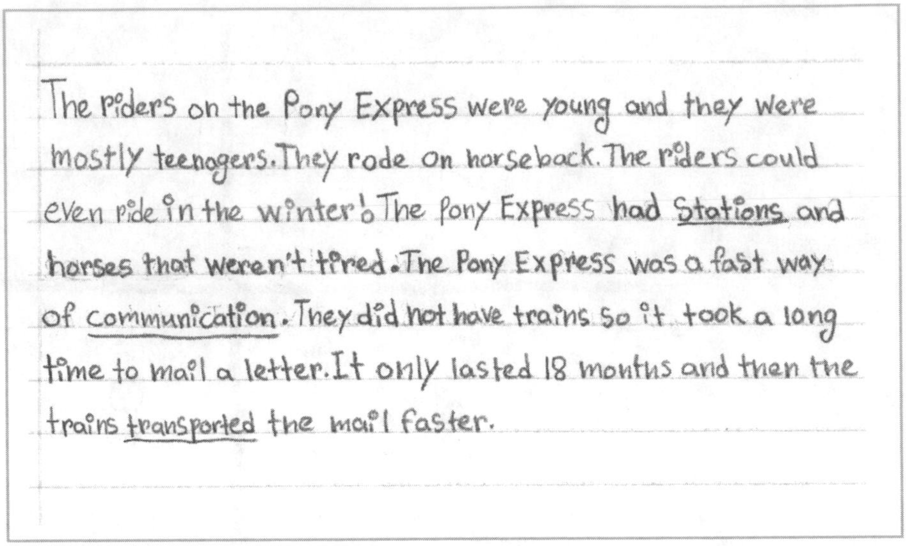

> The riders on the Pony Express were young and they were mostly teenagers. They rode on horseback. The riders could even ride in the winter. The Pony Express had <u>Stations</u> and horses that weren't tired. The Pony Express was a fast way of <u>communication</u>. They did not have trains so it took a long time to mail a letter. It only lasted 18 months and then the trains <u>transported</u> the mail faster.

Figure 6.3 *Tricia's writing with words of the week identified*

The Cumulative Effects of Lots of Reading Experiences

Contact with print has a cumulative effect as the reader encounters known and unknown words. Consider the findings regarding the average number of words learned over the course of school year, which far exceed the amount taught through direct instruction. You'll recall that by some estimates, students working at grade level learn about 3,000 new words per year (White, Graves, and Slater 1990), although only 300 to 500 can be reasonably taught directly (Mason et al. 2003). These same authors applied a simple algorithm to project the number of new words a well-read student (defined as one who reads sixty minutes per day, five days a week) would learn over the course of the year. That theoretical learner would encounter 2,250,000 words per year, of which approximately 2 percent to 5 percent would be unfamiliar to the reader. (This figure is derived from accepted understandings of what constitutes an independent level of reading.) Given that readers permanently acquire knowledge of 5 percent to 10 percent of those unknown words (Nagy and Herman 1987), Mason et al. (2003) estimated that this student would learn at least 2,250 new words per year. And Adams (1990) noted:

> While affirming the value of classroom instruction in vocabulary, we must also recognize its limitations. By our best estimates, the growth in recognition vocabulary of the school age child typically exceeds 3,000 words per year, or

more than eight per day. This order of growth cannot be ascribed to their classroom instruction, nor could it be attained through any feasible program of classroom instruction. (172)

Of course, teachers also know that you can't count on students reading for an hour a day, every day. Although this habit is vital for building background knowledge and vocabulary knowledge (Marzano 2004), students come to our classrooms exhibiting a disparate range of exposure to print. A widely cited study of the reading habits of fifth graders outside the school day found that this range varied from zero to ninety minutes per day, when all text was accounted for (Anderson, Wilson, and Fielding 1988). On average, these students read for thirteen minutes daily, or just over six hundred thousand words per year. Many schools have responded to this unequal distribution of reading experiences by fostering wide reading through sustained silent reading (SSR) and independent reading programs. Incidental vocabulary learning through wide reading has many benefits, as do research-based practices for successful SSR and independent reading programs. Taken schoolwide, these practices become additional tools for fostering word learning.

Considering Wide Reading

Wide reading serves as a useful umbrella term for a host of reading programs and approaches that seek to foster reading habits among students. Learners who read widely, that is, from a broad range of texts, read for a variety of purposes. They seek information, entertainment, and diversion from print and digital sources. This includes books, of course, but also newspapers, comic books, websites, graphic novels, pamphlets, and virtually any other print matter you can imagine.

Wide reading has most commonly been associated with education in Great Britain, Australia, and New Zealand, where students participate in wide reading courses designed to encourage a richer reading diet by extending their exposure to genres and texts. Some of these programs once focused exclusively on canonical literature (the classics), but many now seek to interest and motivate students through practices that allow learners to develop a growing sense of self-awareness as readers. In the United States, wide reading refers to the in- and out-of-school practices of learners who engage with a variety of genres. In-school approaches to wide reading include SSR, which allows for student choice in what is read, and independent reading, where students are given blocks of uninterrupted time to read assigned material.

Learning Vocabulary from Wide Reading

The debate for many years on vocabulary development was whether one learned more effectively from definitional instruction or from context. One camp posited that learning formal definitions was the best way, while others claimed that you needed to learn contextually, that is, through instruction that highlighted the use of a term within a sentence or paragraph. Let's take the word *amused*, which was one of the words Nancy and Sabrina used in their discussion about muses. Those who favored definitional instruction would assert that the best way would be for Sabrina to learn that this word is an adjective that means pleasantly entertained. They would favor instruction that included its use in a sentence: *The children were* amused *when the clown did tricks*. Others would argue that Sabrina should learn the word through context—through the reading of a longer piece of text that utilized this term. As you can probably guess, we think that both are critical to improving students' vocabulary knowledge.

Although acquisition of many words is incidental, there are factors working in the readers' favor. A meta-analysis of twenty studies on vocabulary learning during reading found that students in upper grade levels, those who read more proficiently, and those who possessed some

Reading and applying word knowledge

partial word knowledge of unfamiliar terms were likely to successfully learn up to 15 percent of those new words, if the text wasn't exceedingly difficult (Swanborn and deKlopper 1999). Those are a lot of qualifications, but they serve as a bellwether for educators who are establishing wide reading programs to support vocabulary development. Swanborn and deKlopper (1999) noted the following:

- In order for students to benefit, the text needs to be instructionally useful and not too difficult.

- Older readers overall make larger strides than young children, most likely because they can call upon a larger cache of strategies for approaching unfamiliar words.

- The new words they are most likely to learn are the ones that they know a little bit about.

- The stronger readers are going to make larger gains in vocabulary acquisition than the less proficient ones.

Incidental Vocabulary Learning

As noted earlier, wide reading is of educational interest in part because of the connection to incidental vocabulary learning. Learning becomes incidental when it occurs as an unplanned (although not necessarily unintentional) event. Consider your own incidental learning as you watched someone complete a task like preparing a turkey for a Thanksgiving dinner. In all likelihood, you not only learned how to prepare and baste the turkey, but you also picked up a few other hints along the way, such as the best technique for lifting it out of the roasting pan without dropping it or burning yourself. Incidental learning is a vital part of the learning design of simulations because marshaling complex tasks can't be effectively taught in a strictly linear fashion. At some point, one has to consolidate a variety of skills into a seamless effort. Reading, for instance, occurs in this way. At some point, the reader brings together her knowledge of symbols, sounds, syntax, semantics, and pragmatics and applies this knowledge to new texts.

At the same time, that reader is growing her knowledge of reading by picking up helpful insights along the way. Stanovich (1986) has a term for this: the *Matthew effects* of reading, named after the passage in the Bible's book of Matthew about the rich getting richer. Learners who read more get better at reading because of the incidental learning that occurs and therefore read even more.

Stanovich's findings capture another essential factor in incidental learning: motivation. It appears that occurrences of incidental learning rise as motivation and interest increase. The turkey example is illustrative: your ability to notice details, pick up tips for success, and learn from someone else's mistakes increases if you are intrinsically interested in food preparation, or if you know that you will soon need to be able to do this yourself. Incidental learning of vocabulary occurs in much the same way. Readers who are interested in the topic at hand are likely to pick up more vocabulary along the way. Most of us have witnessed this in a young child with a deep interest in dinosaurs, let's say. We marvel in his ability to spout off terms like *oviraptor* and *allosaurus* and correctly identify them in an illustration. In this case, the child's interest in the topic contributes to his incidental learning of this technical vocabulary.

Incidental learning increases when students are motivated and interested. In particular, their motivation is directed by their own goals for completing the reading (Guthrie and Wigfield 2000). These goals might

Focus on Struggling Readers

Wide reading allows the learner to explore texts *that meet his needs and interests*. To help our struggling readers, we can never lose sight of the role of true choice in motivating children to do the hard work of reading. Many struggling readers have a tough time knowing what a just-right book is, and we have to confer with them one-on-one often to help them learn to find books at their level. But that said, don't limit them to books at their reading level. Give them the dignity of learning about themselves as readers and as people by trying on lots of books. While every book won't be a perfect fit, they will never learn that without experience. Use one-on-one reading conferences as the forum to discover their interests, and show them strategies that can help them learn from books beyond their reading level. For example, many nonfiction books have photos and captions, sidebars, and visual information that a struggling reader can enjoy and learn from, even if she isn't able to read the book cover to cover. When children read about topics they are passionate about, they can carry important background knowledge from one book to another, which helps them build their vocabularies.

include learning how to do something, being entertained, or acquiring more information about a topic of interest. For teachers, this can be a challenge at times. Topics of interest to our students may not resonate with us. Therefore, knowing something about their interests is an important first step in acquiring reading materials for them to use.

Approaches to Wide Reading

Exposure to lots of reading material is an important component in a program to develop subject area vocabulary, especially because of its contributions to building background knowledge (Marzano 2004) and incidental vocabulary learning (Swanborn and deKlopper 1999). Two such efforts that provide students opportunities to extend their vocabulary knowledge are sustained silent reading and independent reading.

Sustained Silent Reading— Getting Hooked on the Reading Habit

Sustained silent reading is dedicated time set aside for students to read what they choose. It is designed to build reading habits, background knowledge, and vocabulary. As such, there is evidence that SSR contributes to students' positive attitudes toward reading (Yoon 2002). In addition, SSR has been found to be a contributory factor in positive achievements in school reform (Fisher 2004; Mosenthal et al. 2004). A comparative study of seventh- and eighth-grade students found that those who participated in an SSR program showed larger gains in vocabulary than those who received regular reading instruction alone (Holt and O'Tuel 1989).

We can't proceed in the conversation about SSR without addressing the National Reading Panel report (NRP 2000). The urban legend surrounding this report is that the NRP said that in-school free reading programs don't work. However, that is a misinterpretation of the panel's report on fluency instruction, which states that while it was unable to draw a recommendation from the 14 studies it examined (from a pool of 603), it did recommend that further research be conducted (NRP 2000). What remains in evidence is a large body of research that the NRP was unable to consider because of its restrictive statistical methodology requirements. The report did not recommend, however, the suspension of wide reading at school.

AN EFFECTIVE SSR PROGRAM   The work of Janice Pilgreen (2000) has been instrumental in the success of SSR programs across the country. She performed a meta-analysis of several studies on SSR to determine which factors contributed to a successful program. She found that there was a modest increase in reading achievement with SSR and a statistically significant effect on interest and motivation toward reading. These are the eight factors she identified:

- *Access*: Students need to be flooded with reading materials.

- *Appeal*: The reading materials should be geared toward the interests of the students who are reading them.

- *Conducive Environment*: The physical setting should be quiet and comfortable.

- *Encouragement*: Students need supportive adult role models who can offer assistance in locating reading materials.

- *Staff Training*: SSR doesn't just happen; the staff of a school should be well versed in the goals and procedures used at the school.

- *Nonaccountability*: Pilgreen found that students read more, and had more positive attitudes toward reading, when book reports and such were not required. This is perhaps the most controversial factor she discussed.

- *Follow-Up Activities*: Pilgreen did find that follow-up activities such as conversations about books read by students or the teacher encouraged others to try them out.

- *Distributed Time to Read*: A common error made by schools new to SSR is that they have one long period a week, rather than shorter SSR periods that occur daily. Pilgreen found that successful programs allowed children to read for fifteen to twenty minutes daily.

In addition, Marzano (2004) found these factors to be necessary in order to develop a wide reading habit necessary for building background knowledge, and further found that these efforts need to be sustained for a year or more in order for students to reap the benefits. Let's look inside a classroom to see how SSR can be implemented.

As students return from lunch, Max speeds up to enter his sixth-grade classroom before the door closes. "My favorite time," Ms. Carruthers says with a sigh. "Are you ready? Get started!" The students know what to do, since SSR at this school takes place at the same time each day. For twenty minutes, students, teachers, administrators, and noninstructional personnel settle in with a good book (or a host of other reading materials). Some students walk to the back of the class to choose a book from the teacher's collection of SSR materials. There are quite a few items reflecting the individual interests of the classroom teacher, but there are also magazines, newspapers, graphic novels, and trade books. But most students read from their own reading material.

Max picks up a copy of *Ballpark* (Curlee 2005), a nonfiction book about America's baseball fields. He first thumbs through the glossy illustrations and starts to read. As he reads the following passage, he uses his problem-solving strategies to figure out some of the vocabulary:

> When the war was over, baseball confronted the worst of America—the festering issue of race. After DiMaggio and Williams and all the other war veterans returned to the game in 1946, it seemed as though things would return to the way they had always been. But one of the club owners decided the time was right for change. Branch Rickey of the Brooklyn Dodgers courageously defied the unspoken rule and hired an African American to play major-league baseball. Jackie Robinson was a military veteran and a superb all-around athlete. Handsome, with immense personal dignity and charisma, he had a scrappy, daring style of play. Rickey felt that Robinson would be a great asset to the club, and he was right. (24)

Max uses his background knowledge on baseball to understand use of terms like *major-league* and *club*. However, two words cause him to stumble. *Festering* is unfamiliar to him. He has heard the word *fester* but doesn't know what it means. He thinks about the sentence and the author's use of the phrase *confronted the worst*. He also remembers that people weren't always treated fairly and recalls reading *Bud, Not Buddy* (Curtis 1999) last year, which hinted at race conflict in 1936. *Maybe there's a link there*, he thinks. It might be something worth paying attention to, like the conflict is still continuing in 1946, ten years later. He rereads, substituting the word *continuing*, and is satisfied with the meaning. While he hasn't determined exactly the right meaning and still lacks an understanding of *festering*, his substitution does not prevent him from understanding the passage.

The other problem word is *charisma*. Max knows that the word is being used to describe Jackie Robinson and that it's a positive term, but he writes it in his vocabulary journal as a word to learn more about later.

Max continues to read until the chime signaling the end of SSR sounds twenty minutes later. As he puts his book back in his desk, he catches his teacher's eye and says, "Good book—you should read it." He then opens his student dictionary to find the word *charisma* and learns that it is, in fact, a positive term meaning that the person can inspire

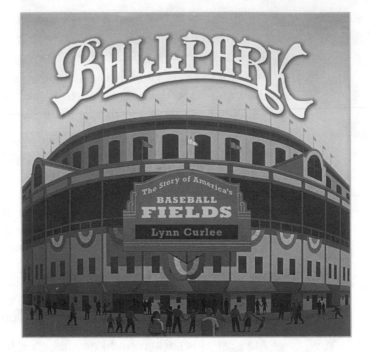

others. Max makes a note to himself, "Yes, Jackie Robinson has charisma and maybe I will, too."

Independent Reading— Applying What Is Known in Content Texts

Independent reading differs from sustained silent reading in one key regard—the amount of choice. Students participating in SSR select texts from a host of materials, including those that are not directly related to a content area. Students engaged in independent reading choose reading materials from those selected by the teacher based on the content or topic under investigation.

The ability to read longer texts in order to support one's learning becomes critical as students enter the intermediate grades. As subject matter becomes more complex, it becomes necessary to assign reading in order for learners to acquire a broader and deeper knowledge of the topic. The amount of assigned reading rises rapidly in postsecondary schooling, and college students are expected to read outside of class. Most of us recall the daunting reading lists we received with our syllabi in our undergraduate courses.

In elementary school, the amount of time allotted to independent reading of content material varies widely. For some teachers, independent reading is connected to a research project or specific unit of study.

For others, it's a way to build background knowledge in science and social studies. In any case, the conditions for learning described in earlier chapters apply to independent reading. They include the following:

- *Choice*: Students' ability to exercise some choice contributes to their learning.

- *Relevance*: The texts identified must be perceived as useful to the learner, often through completion of a task.

- *Differentiation*: The average classroom is attended by a range of students who read anywhere from several years below grade level to high school level. The range of readability of assigned materials should coincide with the range of learners. And remember, students do not acquire vocabulary from texts that are too difficult (Swanborn and deKlopper 1999).

Some teachers may need to broaden their definition of what constitutes content reading material. We include picture books, compilations of previously published articles, photo-essays, newspapers and magazines, and Web-based readings. By using richly detailed source materials such as these, we are able to meet the conditions described above. These reading materials are especially valuable in courses like social studies and science, where timely information is essential to supplement textbooks written and published years earlier. Let's look at how two students confirm and expand their vocabulary knowledge through independent reading.

The students in Mr. Jacobson's fifth-grade science class have been conducting research on the contributions of important scientists. He has assembled a number of reading materials to address the range of readers in his class (see Figure 6.4 for a list of some of the titles he featured in his class). These books collectively also are serving to build his students' background knowledge as they each read several books during the unit.

Saamiya, who reads above grade level, has been reading *Who Was Charles Darwin?* (Hopkinson 2005) and has enjoyed the recounting of Darwin's trip on the *HMS Beagle* as he sailed around Cape Horn and up to the Galapagos. She read the following passage about his work after the trip:

> The word *theory* has two meanings, which we can think of as "little-t theory" and "big-T Theory." At this point, Charles' theory was a "little-t theory." It was a hunch that needed to be tested. In other words, Charles "species theory" was his ideas about evolution by natural selection. (72)

Birch, B. 1996. *Pasteur's Fight Against Microbes*. Hauppauge, NY: Barrons.

Bolden, T. 2008. *George Washington Carver*. New York: Harry N. Abrams.

Brallier, J. 2002. *Who Was Albert Einstein?* New York: Grosset and Dunlap.

Dortey, J. 2007. *DK Eyewitness Book: Great Scientists*. London: DK.

Hopkinson, D. 2005. *Who Was Charles Darwin?* New York: Grosset and Dunlap.

McClafferty, C. K. 2006. *Something Out of Nothing: Marie Curie and Radium*. New York: Farrar, Straus, and Giroux.

Murphy, P. J. 2004. *Grace Hopper: Computer Whiz*. Berkeley Heights, NJ: Enslow Elementary.

Zannos, S. 2004. *The Life and Times of Archimedes*. Hockessin, DE: Mitchell Lane.

Figure 6.4 *Books about scientists*

Saamiya paused to think about the definitional context clue the author had embedded into the paragraph. Although she didn't label it in this way, she realized that she should notice both the definition and the clarification of the term *theory*, a Tier 3 word (specific to a discipline; see Chapter 1). She read on and, at the end of the next paragraph, encountered this sentence: "A 'big-T Theory' is a group of ideas, rules, or principles that explains why or how something happens" (73). This confirmed her emerging understanding of *theory*. She placed a sticky note on the page and wrote "definition of theory" because she expected that she would need this for her report.

Meanwhile, Aaron, who reads a bit below grade level, has selected *George Washington Carver* (Bolden 2008), especially because he is intrigued by the photographs featured in this picture book. Although the text may be a little difficult for him, he brings a great deal of interest and background knowledge to the topic. His grandfather, a devoted gardener, has told Aaron quite a bit about Carver and his connection to his alma mater, Iowa State University. Aaron read this section about Carver's education:

> At Iowa Agricultural College and Model Farm, Carver excelled in horticulture as well as botany (the study of plant life). In class after class, he made his professors proud, especially Louis Pammel, an expert in mycology (the study of fungi such as mushrooms), and a pioneer in ecology (the study of the interrelatedness of the vegetable, mineral, and animal worlds). Professor Pammel wanted Carver to add a master's to his bachelor's degree (which he earned in 1894).

When Carver agreed, the college made him an assistant professor of botany. (17)

Like Saamiya, Aaron is able to use the embedded definitions of branches of natural science to understand that Carver's professor knew a lot about plants. When he reads the sentence about Carver's faculty position, Aaron rereads the definition of *botany* at the beginning of the paragraph. Although the text is complex, Aaron is able to connect this to his background knowledge about Carver's life to question whether his grandfather's story was accurate. He then looks more closely at the photograph on the same page, a class picture. His eyes light up when he reads, "Carver (back row) in Creamery Operators class, circa 1894, at what is now Iowa State University, where he was the first black student and professor" (17). Grandpa was right!

■ The Takeaway

Schoolwide initiatives raise word consciousness among teachers and students because they communicate the powerful message that words matter. One such program is Words of the Week, which focuses on a small group of semantically and structurally related words. The purpose has less to do with memorizing the exact definitions of these words and more to do with highlighting the meaning pattern present in the group so that students can apply the pattern to unfamiliar words.

Another schoolwide vocabulary initiative is a commitment to wide reading. Wide reading is an important component in an intentional vocabulary program, although it should be clear that it does not replace direct instruction through teacher modeling. Nor should it be used as a substitute for the learning activities that foster peer interactions to build knowledge or individual learning through meaningful work with words. However, wide reading through SSR and independent reading allows students to extend their vocabulary learning with texts that build background knowledge and challenge them to apply word knowledge to new forms of information. We advocate for wide reading to be integrated into a larger overall initiative of vocabulary development that occurs across all content areas. Reading is a fundamental element to subject matter learning, and reading texts that extend that learning are beneficial for all.

CHAPTER

7

Make It Your Own

How to Keep Learning About
Academic Vocabulary

By now, you're probably asking yourself, *How can I summarize and synthesize all of the information I've read in this book?* We know that the information we've shared in these pages can be a bit overwhelming. We don't know anyone (including ourselves) who does all of these things on a daily basis. That really would be overwhelming and would prevent students from doing anything else!

We do know teachers, however, who focus regularly on academic vocabulary. We see it in their classrooms and in the performance of their students. In this final chapter, we'd like to provide some concluding thoughts and some additional resources we have found helpful in improving our academic vocabulary instruction. Figure 7.1 provides an overview of these lessons.

Things to Avoid	Things to Do More
• Neglect vocabulary	• Understand the difference between general, specialized, and technical vocabulary
• Teach one definition of a word	• Purposefully select academic vocabulary words for instruction
• Require that students look up word meanings in a dictionary	• Model vocabulary solving, especially using context clues, word parts, and resources
• Assess words out of context, especially with single definitions for words	• Provide students opportunities for peer interaction with the expectation that they will *use* their developing academic vocabulary
	• Examine students' academic vocabulary work for reteaching opportunities
	• Ensure that students read widely on a daily basis

Figure 7.1 *What we've learned about effective vocabulary instruction*

■ Lessons Learned

Having transformed from teachers who taught vocabulary through telling into teachers who purposefully integrate academic vocabulary instruction into our classrooms, we've learned some things along the way. First, and most importantly, word selection is critical. Knowing the types of words students use and what words they need to learn helps in the selection process. In addition, selecting words with colleagues who teach the same grade is helpful, yet we've also learned that the targeted academic vocabulary in classrooms may need to differ based on student need. Simply said, teachers must know their students well to make these determinations, and they need to have the chance to make these decisions.

Second, we've learned that many students don't have mental models for solving unknown words. As such, we are big believers in the role that teacher modeling plays in students' academic vocabulary development. That's not to say that we think that students will learn individual words during teacher modeling, but rather that they will learn a procedure for addressing their own vocabulary questions.

Third, we know that students need lots of opportunities to build and consolidate their academic vocabulary. As such, we have to structure classrooms so that students are expected to use the words we teach, both specialized and technical. As we have discussed, peer interaction is critical for vocabulary learning. As teachers, we simply must structure peer conversations and activities if we want to improve student engagement and achievement.

Fourth, we have learned that while modeling and peer interactions are critical components for effective academic vocabulary development, they are not in and of themselves enough to radically change word learning. They are necessary, but not sufficient. Students must consolidate their vocabulary learning during independent activities. And teachers should use this student work as an assessment opportunity, checking for understanding to ensure that students are truly expanding their knowledge.

And finally, we have long understood the importance of wide reading. We all benefit, in countless ways, from wide reading. We gain information and are entertained. And, along the way, we learn new concepts and words. Providing students with a steady diet of reading materials of all sorts ensures that they extend their knowledge of academic vocabulary, even in the absence of the teacher. We have learned through our own wide reading that there are excellent resources for teaching vocabulary. In the section that follows, we share some of these with you.

■ Teacher Resources for Vocabulary Development

The following list of books is composed of titles we consult on a regular basis. They're the books we go to for answers.

- *The Vocabulary Book: Learning and Instruction*, by Michael F. Graves (2006): This book presents a four-part plan for vocabulary instruction: rich and varied language experiences, teaching individual words, teaching word-learning strategies, and fostering word consciousness. We especially appreciate the way that Graves explains the importance of being word conscious.

- *Teaching Vocabulary in All Classrooms*, by Camille Blachowicz and Peter Fisher (2002): Based on their extensive review of research, Blachowicz and Fisher explain the teaching of vocabulary in a number of categories, including learning vocabulary from context, integrating vocabulary and reading strategy instruction, learning vocabulary in literature-based reading instruction, learning vocabulary in the content areas, using dictionaries and other references, and assessing vocabulary knowledge. We are especially indebted to this book for its focus on wordplay in the classroom.

- *Building Background Knowledge for Academic Achievement*, by Robert Marzano (2004): In one of our favorite books, Marzano makes the case that teachers should focus on wide reading and subject-specific vocabulary. He not only notes the importance of background knowledge in ensuring students are successful in school but also provides classroom examples across elementary, middle, and high school classrooms.

- *Bringing Words to Life: Robust Vocabulary Instruction*, by Isabel Beck, Margaret McKeown, and Linda Kucan (2002): Simply said, no library would be complete without this book. This comprehensive book makes a compelling case for word selection and instructional routines. While we take minor exceptions, we have learned a great deal from this excellent resource.

▪ Classroom Materials for Learning Words Inside and Out

In addition to professional reading materials, we know that classrooms need to have resources for students to continue their word learning. Following are several materials we've found useful in elementary classrooms.

Of course, we can't imagine a classroom without a good dictionary. But perhaps even more important are the growing number of content-specific dictionaries. For example:

- *The American Heritage Science Dictionary* (Editors of the American Heritage Dictionaries 2005)

- *My First Dictionary* (Root 1993)

- *Merriam-Webster Children's Dictionary* (Dorling Kindersley 2008)

- *A Dictionary of Science* (Daintith 2005)

- *The Penguin Dictionary of Mathematics*, 3d ed. (Nelson 2003)

- *The Yale Dictionary of Art and Artists* (Langmuir and Lynton 2000)

Of course, there are a number of online dictionaries available on the Internet that teachers can bookmark. Our classroom computer bookmarks include

- *General Words*: Merriam-Webster: www.m-w.com

- *Visual Dictionary*: www.infovisual.info

- *Rhyming Words (especially those with multiple syllables)*: www.rhymezone.com

- *Spanish Language*: www.spanishdict.com

- *World Languages*: www.wordreference.com

- *Thesaurus*: www.bartleby.com/thesauri

- *Visual Thesaurus*: www.visualthesaurus.com

Using these dictionaries, you can develop favorite activities to do with your students. For example, you can teach students cutting-edge new words by visiting Merriam-Webster's online collegiate dictionary at www.m-w.com/info/new_words.htm (Bromley 2007). Or you might have students use them to play the classic dictionary game, where players take turns finding an obscure dictionary word related to the content area, saying just the word to the other players, and then players write convincing definitions on slips of paper. The player who found the word reads aloud the student definitions along with a slip of paper containing the dictionary definition, and players vote on which one is the real definition. Whichever player garners the most votes wins.

In addition to dictionaries, we strongly recommend the series of books related to vocabulary cartoons. They are easy to use and students enjoy them. But more importantly, students learn from them. For more information about these books, visit www.vocabularycartoons.com.

Even well-read students are confounded at times by idioms, especially those that were popular in an earlier time. We keep a copy of *Webster's New World American Idioms Handbook* (Brenner 2003) available for students to use when they encounter phrases like *loose cannon* or *pardon my French*. Speaking of which, each of us also keeps a copy of the *American Slang Dictionary* (Spears 2006) on our own desk. It does contain vulgar language, so we don't make it available to students, but we find it handy for deciphering the sometimes impenetrable speech of our students.

Idioms and slang are good points for us to end on, because it reminds us that our language is continually shaped by its users. In the same regard, its users influence vocabulary instruction. The needs of learners should determine the best path for instruction, the best alchemy of approaches that foster their academic growth. Teachers who are committed to sharing their content expertise should adapt and improve on the strategies discussed in this book according to their needs.

We've spoken throughout this book about the notion of learning words inside and out. We've explored this phrase in a number of ways, but we'd like to summarize our thinking here. At the surface level, learning words inside and out refers to the need for deep meaning. Students need to know words well. They need to understand the nuances and connotations words have and learn to use precise vocabulary in their speaking and writing.

Second, we presented an approach to figuring out unknown words that also uses an inside-and-out approach. Readers can sometimes figure out words from looking outside of the word and other times from looking inside the word. Through teacher modeling and practice, students learn to use both inside and outside strategies for determining word meanings, especially for unknown words they encounter while reading.

And finally, we know that learning words inside and out can refer to the environments in which students use and learn subject area vocabulary. When our teaching is at its best, our students take what they've learned inside our classrooms to their outside lives. Vocabulary doesn't exist between the school bells—it is carried with each learner for the rest of his or her life.

Appendix: Dolch Word Lists

Pre-primer (40 words)

a	find	is	not	three
and	for	it	one	to
away	funny	jump	play	two
big	go	little	red	up
blue	help	look	run	we
can	here	make	said	where
come	I	me	see	yellow
down	in	my	the	you

Primer (52 words)

all	do	no	she	well
am	eat	now	so	went
are	four	on	soon	what
at	get	our	that	white
ate	good	out	there	who
be	have	please	they	will
black	he	pretty	this	with
brown	into	ran	too	yes
but	like	ride	under	
came	must	saw	want	
did	new	say	was	

First Grade (41 words)

after	fly	how	open	then
again	from	just	over	think
an	give	know	put	walk
any	giving	let	round	were
as	had	live	some	when
ask	has	may	stop	
by	her	of	take	
could	him	old	thank	
every	his	once	them	

Second Grade (46 words)

always	does	made	tell	why
around	don't	many	their	wish
because	fast	off	these	work
been	first	or	those	would
before	five	pull	upon	write
best	found	read	us	your
both	gave	right	use	
buy	goes	sing	very	
call	green	sit	wash	
cold	its	sleep	which	

Third Grade (41 words)

about	eight	if	only	ten
better	fall	keep	own	today
bring	far	kind	pick	together
carry	full	laugh	seven	try
clean	got	light	shall	warm
cut	grow	long	show	
done	hold	much	six	
draw	hot	myself	small	
drink	hurt	never	start	

Nouns (95 words)

apple	children	flower	money	sister
baby	Christmas	game	morning	snow
back	coat	garden	mother	song
ball	corn	girl	name	squirrel
bear	cow	good-bye	nest	stick
bed	day	grass	night	street
bell	dog	ground	paper	sun
bird	doll	hand	party	table
birthday	door	head	picture	thing
boat	duck	hill	pig	time
box	egg	home	rabbit	top
boy	eye	horse	rain	toy
bread	farm	house	ring	tree
brother	farmer	kitty	robin	watch
cake	father	leg	Santa Claus	water
car	feet	letter	school	way
cat	fire	man	seed	wind
chair	fish	men	sheep	window
chicken	floor	milk	shoe	wood

References

Chapter 1

ANDREASEN, D. 2008. *The Giant of Seville.* New York: Harry N. Abrams.

BAKER, S. K., D. C. SIMMONS, AND E. J. KAME'ENUI. 1998. "Vocabulary Acquisition: Research Bases." In *What Reading Research Tells Us About Children with Diverse Learning Needs,* ed. D. C. Simmons and E. J. Kame'enui, 183–218. Mahwah, NJ: Lawrence Erlbaum.

BECK, I. L., M. G. McKEOWN, AND L. KUCAN. 2002. *Bring Words to Life: Robust Vocabulary Instruction.* New York: Guilford.

CANTRELL, S. C. 1999. "The Effects of Literacy Instruction on Primary Students' Reading and Writing Achievement." *Reading Research and Instruction* 39 (1): 3–26.

CRONBACH, L. J. 1942. "An Analysis of Techniques for Systematic Vocabulary Testing." *Journal of Educational Research* 36: 206–17.

DALE, E., J. O'ROURKE, AND H. A. BAMMAN. 1971. *Techniques for Teaching Vocabulary.* Palo Alto, CA: Field Educational Publications.

EDWARDS, J. A., AND E. W. HAMILTON. 2006. *The Great American Mousical.* New York: HarperCollins.

FISHER, D., AND N. FREY. 2007. "Implementing a Schoolwide Literacy Framework: Improving Achievement in an Urban Elementary School." *The Reading Teacher* 61: 32–45.

———. 2008. *Better Learning Through Structured Teaching: A Framework for the Gradual Release of Responsibility.* Alexandria, VA: Association for Supervision and Curriculum Development.

FRANCIS, M. A., AND M. L. SIMPSON. 2003. "Using Theory, Our Intuitions, and a Research Study to Enhance Student's Vocabulary Knowledge." *Journal of Adolescent and Adult Literacy* 47: 66–78.

GRAVES, M. F. 1986. "Vocabulary Learning and Instruction." *Review of Educational Research* 13: 49–89.

GRAVES, M. F. 2006. *The Vocabulary Book: Learning and Instruction*. New York: Teachers College.

HATANO, G., AND K. IGNAKI. 1986. "Two Courses of Expertise." In *Child Development and Education in Japan*, ed. H. Stevenson, H. Azuma, and K. Hakuta, 262–72. New York: W. H. Freeman.

KNOWLTON, J. 1997. *Geography from A to Z: A Picture Glossary*. New York: Harper Trophy.

NAGY, W. E., AND R. C. ANDERSON. 1984. "How Many Words Are There in Printed School English?" *Reading Research Quarterly* 19: 303–30.

NATIONAL RESEARCH COUNCIL. 1999. *How People Learn: Brain, Mind, Experience, and School*. Ed. J. D. Bransford, A. L. Brown, and R. R. Cocking. Committee on Developments in Science of Learning. Washington, DC: National Academy Press.

PATCHETT, A. 2005. *Bel Canto*. New York: Harper Perennial.

SCARBOROUGH, H. S. 2001. "Connecting Early Language and Literacy to Later Reading (Dis)abilities: Evidence, Theory, and Practice." In *Handbook for Research in Early Literacy*, ed. S. Neuman and D. Dickinson, 97–110. New York: Guilford.

SCOTT, J. A., D. JAMIESON-NOEL, AND M. ASSELIN. 2003. "Vocabulary Instruction Throughout the Day in Twenty-Three Canadian Upper-Elementary Classrooms." *The Elementary School Journal* 103: 269–86.

STEVENS, R. J. 2006. "Integrated Middle School Literacy Instruction." *Middle School Journal* 38 (1): 13–19.

VACCA, R. T., AND J. A. VACCA. 2007. *Content Area Reading: Literacy and Learning Across the Curriculum*. 9th ed. Boston: Allyn and Bacon.

■ Chapter 2

ADAMS, M. J., AND M. K. HENRY. 1997. "Myths and Realities About Words and Literacy." *School Psychology Review* 26: 425–36.

ALLEN, T. B. 2004. *George Washington, Spymaster: How the Americans Outspied the British and Won the Revolutionary War*. Washington, DC: National Geographic.

BAUMANN, J. F., G. FONT, E. C. EDWARDS, AND E. BOLAND. 2005. "Strategies for

Teaching Middle-Grade Students to Use Word-Part and Context Clues to Expand Reading Vocabulary." In *Teaching and Learning Vocabulary: Bringing Research to Practice*, ed. E. H. Hiebert and M. L. Kamil, 179–205. Mahwah, NJ: Lawrence Erlbaum.

BEAR, D. R., M. INVERNIZZI, S. TEMPLETON, AND F. JOHNSTON. 2008. *Words Their Way: Word Study for Phonics, Vocabulary, and Spelling Instruction.* Upper Saddle River, NJ: Pearson Prentice Hall.

BECK, I. L., M. G. MCKEOWN, AND L. KUCAN. 2002. *Bring Words to Life: Robust Vocabulary Instruction.* New York: Guilford.

CALIFORNIA DEPARTMENT OF EDUCATION. 2000. *Science Content Standards for California Public Schools: Kindergarten Through Grade 12.* Sacramento, CA: author.

CARLE, E. 1970. *The Very Hungry Caterpillar.* New York: World.

COXHEAD, A. 2000. "A New Academic Word List." *TESOL Quarterly* 34 (2): 213–38.

FISHER, D., J. FLOOD, D. LAPP, AND N. FREY. 2004. "Interactive Read Alouds: Is There a Common Set of Implementation Practices?" *The Reading Teacher* 58: 8–17.

FISHER, D., C. ROTHENBERG, AND N. FREY. 2007. *Language Learners in the English Classroom.* Urbana, IL: National Council of Teachers of English.

FRAYER, D. A., W. C. FREDERICK, AND H. J. KLAUSMEIER. 1969. *A Schema for Testing the Level of Concept Mastery.* Working Paper No. 16. Madison: Wisconsin Research and Development Center for Cognitive Learning.

FRY, E. B. 2004. *The Vocabulary Teacher's Book of Lists.* San Francisco: Jossey-Bass.

GRAVES, M. F. 2006. *The Vocabulary Book: Learning and Instruction.* New York: Teachers College.

KRULL, K. 1998. *Lives of the Presidents: Fame, Shame (and What the Neighbors Thought).* San Diego: Harcourt.

MARZANO, R. J. 2004. *Building Background Knowledge for Academic Achievement: Research on What Works in Schools.* Alexandria, VA: Association for Supervision and Curriculum Development.

MARZANO, R. J., AND D. J. PICKERING. 2005. *Building Academic Vocabulary: Teacher's Manual.* Alexandria, VA: Association for Supervision and Curriculum Development.

MONTGOMERY, S. 1999. *The Snake Scientist.* New York: Houghton Mifflin.

NAGY, W. E. 1988. *Teaching Vocabulary to Improve Reading Comprehension.* Urbana, IL: National Council of Teachers of English.

NAGY, W. E., AND P. A. HERMAN. 1987. "Breadth and Depth of Vocabulary Knowledge: Implications for Acquisition and Instruction." In *The Nature of Vocabulary Acquisition,* ed. M. G. McKeown and M. E. Curtis, 19–36. Hillsdale, NJ: Lawrence Erlbaum.

NETTLETON, P. H. 2004. *Think, Think, Think: Learning About Your Brain.* Minneapolis, MN: Picture Window Books.

OGDEN, C. K. 1930. *Basic English: A General Introduction with Rules and Grammar.* London: Paul Treber.

PEARSON, P. D., AND G. GALLAGHER. 1983. "The Gradual Release of Responsibility Model of Instruction." *Contemporary Educational Psychology* 8: 112–23.

POLLARD-DURODOLA, S. D., P. G. MATHES, AND S. VAUGHN. 2006. "The Role of Oracy in Developing Comprehension in Spanish-Speaking English Language Learners." *Topics in Language Disorders* 26: 365–84.

SIMON, S. 1997. *The Brain: Our Nervous System.* New York: HarperCollins.

STAHL, S. A., AND M. M. FAIRBANKS. 1986. "The Effects of Vocabulary Instruction: A Model-Based Meta-Analysis." *Review of Educational Research* 56 (1): 72–110.

WHITE, T. G., J. SOWELL, AND A. YANAGIHARA. 1989. "Teaching Elementary Students to Use Word-Part Clues." *The Reading Teacher* 42: 302–308.

WIGGINS, G., AND J. MCTIGHE. 2005. *Understanding by Design.* 2d ed. Alexandria, VA: Association for Supervision and Curriculum Development.

■ Chapter 3

AFFLERBACH, P., AND P. JOHNSTON. 1984. "On the Use of Verbal Reports in Reading Research." *Journal of Reading Behavior* 16: 307–22.

BARCLAY, K., AND L. TRASER. 1999. "Supporting Young Researchers as They Learn to Write." *Childhood Education* 75: 215–24.

BECK, I. L., M. G. MCKEOWN, AND L. KUCAN. 2002. *Bringing Words to Life: Robust Vocabulary Instruction.* New York: Guilford.

BECK, I. L., M. G. MCKEOWN, AND E. S. MCCASLIN. 1983. "Vocabulary Development: All Contexts Are Not Created Equal." *The Elementary School Journal* 83: 177–81.

BEREITER, C., AND M. BIRD. 1985. "Use of Thinking Aloud in Identification and Teaching of Reading Comprehension Strategies." *Cognition and Instruction* 2: 131–56.

BLACHOWICZ, C., AND P. FISHER. 2005. *Teaching Vocabulary in All Classrooms*. 3d ed. Upper Saddle River, NJ: Pearson Merrill Prentice Hall.

BOLDEN, T. 2008. *George Washington Carver*. New York: Harry N. Abrams.

BURNFORD, S. 1960. *The Incredible Journey*. New York: Bantam Books.

CRONIN, D. 2000. *Click, Clack, Moo: Cows That Type*. New York: Simon and Schuster.

DAVEY, B. 1983. "Think Aloud: Modeling the Cognitive Processes of Reading Comprehension." *Journal of Reading* 27: 44–47.

DUFFY, G. G. 2003. *Explaining Reading: A Resource for Teaching Concepts, Skills, and Strategies*. New York: Guilford.

FARNDON, J. 2007. *Extreme Weather*. New York: Dorling Kindersley.

FISHER, D., AND N. FREY. 2008. *Better Learning Through Structured Teaching: A Framework for the Gradual Release of Responsibility*. Alexandria, VA: Association for Supervision and Curriculum Development.

FISHER, D., N. FREY, AND D. LAPP. 2008. "Shared Reading: Teaching Comprehension, Vocabulary, Text Structures, and Text Features." *The Reading Teacher* 61: 548–57.

GORE, A. 2007. *An Inconvenient Truth: The Crisis of Global Warming (Adapted for a New Generation)*. New York: Penguin.

ISDELL, W. 1993. *A Gebra Named Al*. Minneapolis, MN: Free Spirit.

MARTIN, B., AND J. ARCHAMBAULT. 1987. *Knots on a Counting Rope*. New York: Henry Holt.

RECKSIEK, J. 2005. "Benefits of Teacher Modeling of Reading and Literature Discussion Groups in a Fifth-Grade Classroom." *Essays in Education* 13: 1–9.

WILFORD, S. 2007. "Modeling Appropriate Behaviors: Helping Teachers Recognize Their Position as Role Models for Children." *Early Childhood Today* 21 (5): 8–9.

WILHELM, J. 2001. *Improving Comprehension with Think-Aloud Strategies: Modeling What Good Readers Do*. New York: Scholastic.

■ Chapter 4

ANDERS, P., AND C. BOS. 1986. "Semantic Feature Analysis: An Interactive Strategy for Vocabulary Development and Text Comprehension." *Journal of Reading* 29: 610–16.

ALVERMANN, D. E., AND P. R. BOOTHBY. 1982. *A Strategy for Making Content Reading Successful: Grades 4–6*. Paper presented at the annual meeting of the Plains Regional Conference of the International Reading Association, Omaha, NE, September.

ARONSON, J., N. BLANEY, C. STEPHIN, J. SIKES, AND M. SNAPP. 1978. *The Jigsaw Classroom*. Beverly Hills, CA: Sage.

BAUMANN, J. F., L. A. JONES, AND N. SEIFERT-KESSELL. 1993. "Using Think Alouds to Enhance Children's Comprehension Monitoring Abilities." *The Reading Teacher* 47: 184–93.

BECK, I. L., M. G. McKEOWN, AND L. KUCAN. 2002. *Bringing Words to Life: Robust Vocabulary Instruction*. New York: Guilford.

BURKE, J. 2002. *Tools for Thought: Graphic Organizers for Your Classroom*. Portsmouth, NH: Heinemann.

CAZDEN, C. B. 1986. "Classroom Discourse." In *Handbook of Research on Teaching*, 3d ed., ed. M. Wittrock, 432–63. New York: Macmillan.

———. 2001. *Classroom Discourse: The Language of Teaching and Learning*. 2d ed. Portsmouth, NH: Heinemann.

CUNNINGHAM, P. 2000. *Systematic Sequential Phonics They Can Use: For Beginning Readers of All Ages*. Greensboro, NC: Carson-Dellosa.

DYKSTRA, P. 1994. "Say It, Don't Write It: Oral Structures as Framework for Teaching Writing." *Journal of Basic Writing* 13 (1): 41–49.

FARNDON, J. 2007. *Extreme Weather*. New York: Dorling Kindersley.

FISHER, A. L. 2001. "Implementing Graphic Organizer Notebooks: The Art and Science of Teaching Content." *The Reading Teacher* 55: 116–20.

FISHER, D., AND N. FREY. 2007. *Improving Adolescent Literacy: Content Area Strategies at Work*. 2d ed. Upper Saddle River, NJ: Pearson Merrill Prentice Hall.

GOODMAN, L. 2004. "Shades of Meaning: Relating and Expanding Word Knowledge." In *Teaching Vocabulary: 50 Creative Strategies, Grades K–12*, ed. G. E. Tompkins and C. Blanchfield, 85–87. Upper Saddle River, NJ: Merrill Prentice Hall.

HATKOFF, I., C. HATKOFF, AND P. KAHUMBU. 2006. *Owen and Mzee: The True Story of a Remarkable Friendship*. New York: Scholastic.

HOHN, R. L., AND B. FREY. 2002. "Heuristic Training and Performance in Elementary Mathematical Problem Solving." *Journal of Educational Research* 95: 374–80.

IVES, B. 2007. "Graphic Organizers Applied to Secondary Algebra Instruction for Students with Learning Disorders." *Learning Disabilities Research and Practice* 22: 110–18.

JOHNSON, D. W., R. T. JOHNSON, AND K. SMITH. 1991. *Active Learning: Cooperation in the College Classroom.* Edina, MN: Interaction Book Co.

KAGAN, S. 1989. *Cooperative Learning Resources for Teachers.* San Juan Capistrano, CA: Resources for Teachers.

LOWRY, L. 1993. *The Giver.* New York: Bantam Doubleday Dell.

LYMAN, F. 1987. "Think-Pair-Share: An Expanding Teaching Technique." *MAA-CIE Cooperative News* 1: 1–2.

MACLACHLAN, P. 1985. *Sarah, Plain and Tall.* New York: HarperTrophy.

MCCAGG, E., AND D. DANSEREAU. 1991. "A Convergent Paradigm for Examining Knowledge Mapping as a Learning Strategy." *Journal of Educational Research* 84: 317–24.

MCGINLEY, W. J., AND P. R. DENNER. 1987. "Story Impressions. A Prereading/ Writing Activity." *Journal of Reading* 31: 248–54.

MOUNTAIN, L. 2002. "Flip-a-Chip to Build Vocabulary." *Journal of Adolescent and Adult Literacy* 46: 62–68.

OCZKUS, L. D. 2003. *Reciprocal Teaching at Work: Strategies for Improving Reading Comprehension.* Newark, DE: International Reading Association.

OSTER, L. 2001. "Using the Think-Aloud for Reading Instruction." *The Reading Teacher* 55: 64–69.

PALINCSAR, A. S. 1987. "Reciprocal Teaching: Can Student Discussion Boost Comprehension?" *Instructor* 96 (5): 56–58, 60.

PÉREZ, B. 1996. "Instructional Conversations as Opportunities for English Language Acquisition for Culturally and Linguistically Diverse Students." *Language Arts* 73: 173–81.

PITTELMAN, S. D., J. HEIMLICH, R. BERGLUND, M. FRENCH, AND J. E. HEIMLICH. 1991. *Semantic Feature Analysis: Classroom Application.* Newark, DE: International Reading Association.

RICHEK, M. A. 2005. "Words Are Wonderful: Interactive, Time-Efficient Strategies to Teach the Meaning of Words." *The Reading Teacher* 58: 414–25.

ROBINSON, D. H. 1998. "Graphic Organizers as Aids to Text Learning." *Reading Research and Instruction* 37: 85–105.

ROSENBAUM, C. 2001. "A Word Map for Middle School: A Tool for Effective Vocabulary Instruction." *Journal of Adolescent and Adult Literacy* 45: 44–49.

RUBENSTEIN, R. N., AND D. R. THOMPSON. 2002. "Understanding and Supporting Students' Mathematical Vocabulary Development." *Teaching Children Mathematics* 9: 107–12.

SELVIDGE, E. 2006. "Journey to Egypt: A Board Game." *Montessori Life: A Publication of the American Montessori Society* 18 (4): 36–39.

STAHL, S. A. 1999. *Vocabulary Development*. Newton Upper Falls, MA: Brookline.

WATSON, K. 1980. "A Close Look at Whole-Class Discussion." *English in Education* 14: 39–44.

WILHELM, J. D. 2001. "Think-Alouds Boost Reading Comprehension." *Instructor* 111: 26–28.

■ Chapter 5

ALLEN, J. 2000. *Words, Words, Words: Teaching Vocabulary in Grades 4–12*. York, ME: Stenhouse.

BEAR, D. R., M. INVERNIZZI, S. R. TEMPLETON, AND F. JOHNSTON. 2007. *Words Their Way: Word Study for Phonics, Vocabulary, and Spelling Instruction*. 4th ed. Upper Saddle River, NJ: Prentice Hall.

BLACHOWICZ, C. L. Z., AND P. J. FISHER. 2002. *Teaching Vocabulary in All Classrooms*. 2d ed. Upper Saddle River, NJ: Merrill Prentice Hall.

FEARN, L., AND N. FARNAN. 2001. *Interactions: Teaching Writing and the Language Arts*. Boston: Allyn and Bacon.

FISHER, D., AND N. FREY. 2003. "Writing Instruction for Struggling Adolescent Writers: A Gradual Release Model." *Journal of Adolescent and Adult Literacy* 46: 396–407.

———. 2007. *Scaffolding Writing Instruction: A Gradual Release Model*. New York: Scholastic.

FRAYER, D., W. C. FREDERICK, AND H. J. KLAUSMEIER. 1969. *A Schema for Testing the Level of Cognitive Mastery*. Madison, WI: Center for Education Research.

FREY, N., AND D. FISHER. 2007. *Reading for Information in Elementary School: Content Literacy Strategies to Build Comprehension*. Upper Saddle River, NJ: Merrill Prentice Hall.

Goodwin, L. 2001. "A Tool for Learning: Vocabulary Self-Awareness." In *Creative Vocabulary: Strategies for Teaching Vocabulary in Grades K–12*, ed. C. Blanchfield, 44–46. Fresno, CA: San Joaquin Valley Writing Project.

Graff, G., and C. Birkenstein. 2006. *They Say/I Say: The Moves That Matter in Academic Writing*. New York: W. W. Norton.

Jones, R. C., and T. G. Thomas. 2006. "Leave No Discipline Behind." *The Reading Teacher* 60: 58–64.

Lewis, M., and D. Wray. 1995. *Developing Children's Non-Fiction Writing*. New York: Scholastic.

Munsch, R. N. 1992. *The Paper Bag Princess*. Toronto: Annick.

Murdoch, K., and J. Wilson. 2006. "Student Independent Learning." *Education Quarterly (Australia)*. Retrieved July 5, 2007, from www1.curriculum.edu.au/eq/summer2006/article1.html.

Nagy, W. E. 1988. *Teaching Vocabulary to Improve Reading Instruction*. Newark, DE: International Reading Association.

Paivio, A. 1969. "Mental Imagery in Associative Learning and Memory." *Psychological Review* 3: 241–63.

Pianta, R. C., J. Belsky, R. Houts, and F. Morrison. 2007. "Opportunities to Learn in America's Elementary Classrooms." *Science* 315: 1795–96.

Pressley, M., J. R. Levin, and H. D. Delaney. 1983. "The Mnemonic Keyword Method." *Review of Educational Research* 52: 61–91.

Race, P. 1996. *A Fresh Look at Independent Learning*. Retrieved July 5, 2007, from www.city.londonmet.ac.uk/deliberations/eff.lcarning/indep.html.

Raugh, M. R., and R. C. Atkinson. 1975. "A Mnemonic Method for Learning a Second-Language Vocabulary." *Journal of Educational Psychology* 67 (1): 1–16.

Ridley, D. S., P. A. Schutz, R. S. Glanz, and C. E. Weinstein. 1992. "Self-Regulated Learning: The Interactive Influence of Metacognitive Awareness and Goal-Setting." *Journal of Experimental Education* 60: 293–306.

Ruddell, M. R., and B. A. Shearer. 2002. "'Extraordinary,' 'Tremendous,' 'Exhilarating,' 'Magnificent': Middle School At-Risk Students Become Avid Word Learners with the Vocabulary Self-Collection Strategy (VSS)." *Journal of Adolescent and Adult Literacy* 45: 352–63.

Weber, B. 2004. *Animal Disguises*. Boston: Kingfisher.

▪ Chapter 6

ADAMS, M. J. 1990. *Beginning to Read: Thinking and Learning About Print*. Cambridge, MA: MIT Press.

ADAMS, M. J., AND M. K. HENRY. 1997. "Myths and Realities About Words and Literacy." *School Psychology Review* 26: 425–36.

ANDERSON, R. C., P. T. WILSON, AND L. G. FIELDING. 1988. "Growth in Reading and How Children Spend Their Time Outside of School." *Reading Research Quarterly* 23: 285–303.

BAUMANN, J. F., G. FONT, E. C. EDWARDS, AND E. BOLAND. 2005. "Strategies for Teaching Middle-Grade Students to Use Word-Part and Context Clues to Expand Reading Vocabulary." In *Teaching and Learning Vocabulary: Bringing Research to Practice*, ed. E. H. Hiebert and M. L. Kamil, 179–205. Mahwah, NJ: Lawrence Erlbaum.

BOLDEN, T. 2008. *George Washington Carver*. New York: Harry N. Abrams.

COLLINS, C. 1980. "Sustained Silent Reading: Effects on Teachers' Behaviors and Students' Achievement." *Elementary School Journal* 81: 108–14.

CURLEE, L. 2005. *Ballpark: The Story of America's Baseball Fields*. New York: Simon and Schuster.

CURTIS, C. P. 1999. *Bud, Not Buddy*. New York: Delacorte.

FISHER, D. 2004. "Setting the 'Opportunity to Read' Standard: Resuscitating the SSR Program in an Urban High School." *Journal of Adolescent and Adult Literacy* 48: 138–50.

FISHER, D., AND N. FREY. 2007. "Implementing a Schoolwide Literacy Framework: Improving Achievement in an Urban Elementary School." *The Reading Teacher* 61: 32–43.

FRAYER, D., W. C. FREDERICK, AND H. J. KLAUSMEIER. 1969. *A Schema for Testing the Level of Cognitive Mastery*. Madison: Wisconsin Center for Education Research.

GUTHRIE, J. T., AND A. WIGFIELD. 2000. "Engagement and Motivation in Reading." In *Handbook of Reading Research*, vol. III, ed. M. L. Kamil, P. B. Mosenthal, P. D. Pearson, and R. L. Barr, 403–24. Mahwah, NJ: Lawrence Erlbaum.

HOLT, S. B., AND F. S. O'TUEL. 1989. "The Effect of Sustained Silent Reading and Writing on Achievement and Attitudes of Seventh and Eighth Grade Students Reading Two Years Below Grade Level." *Reading Improvement* 26: 290–97.

HOPKINSON, D. 2005. *Who Was Charles Darwin?* New York: Grosset and Dunlap.

LANGER, J. A. 2001. "Beating the Odds: Teaching Middle and High School Students to Read and Write Well." *American Educational Research Journal* 38: 837–80.

MARZANO, R. J. 2004. *Building Background Knowledge for Academic Achievement: Research on What Works in Schools.* Alexandria, VA: Association for Supervision and Curriculum Development.

MASON, J. M., S. A. STAHL, K. H. AU, AND P. A. HERMAN. 2003. "Reading: Children's Developing Knowledge of Words." In *Handbook of Research on Teaching the English Language Arts*, 2d ed., ed. J. Flood, D. Lapp, J. R. Squire, and J. M. Jensen, 914–30. Mahwah, NJ: Lawrence Erlbaum.

MOSENTHAL, J., M. LIPSON, S. TORNCELLO, B. RUSS, AND J. MEKKELSEN. 2004. "Contexts and Practices of Six Schools Successful in Obtaining Reading Achievement." *Elementary School Journal* 104: 343–67.

NAGY, W. A., AND P. A. HERMAN. 1987. "Breadth and Depth of Vocabulary Knowledge: Implications for Acquisition and Instruction." In *The Nature of Vocabulary Acquisition*, ed. M. G. McKeown and M. E. Curtis, 19–36. Hillsdale, NJ: Lawrence Erlbaum.

NATIONAL READING PANEL (NRP). 2000. *Teaching Children to Read: An Evidence-Based Assessment of the Scientific Literature on Reading and Its Implications for Instruction: Report of the Subgroups.* Washington, DC: National Institute of Child Health and Human Development.

PILGREEN, J. L. 2000. *The SSR Handbook: How to Organize and Manage a Sustained Silent Reading Program.* Portsmouth, NH: Boynton/Cook.

REEVES, D. 2000. *Accountability in Action: A Blueprint for Learning Organizations.* Denver, CO: Advanced Learning Centers.

STANOVICH, K. E. 1986. "Matthew Effects in Reading: Some Consequences of Individual Differences in the Acquisition of Literacy." *Reading Research Quarterly* 21: 360–406.

STANOVICH, K. E., AND A. CUNNINGHAM. 1992. "Studying the Consequences of Literacy Within a Literate Society: The Cognitive Correlates of Print Exposure." *Memory and Language* 20: 51–88.

SWANBORN, M. S. L., AND K. DEKLOPPER. 1999. "Incidental Word Learning While Reading: A Meta-Analysis." *Review of Educational Research* 69: 261–85.

WEITZMAN, J. P., AND R. P. GLASSER. 1999. *You Can't Take a Balloon into the Metropolitan Museum.* New York: Dial Books for Young Readers.

White, T. G., M. F. Graves, and W. H. Slater. 1990. "Growth of Reading Vocabulary in Diverse Elementary Schools: Decoding and Word Meaning." *Journal of Educational Psychology* 82: 281–90.

Yoon, J. 2002. "Three Decades of Sustained Silent Reading: A Meta-Analytic Review of the Effects of SSR on Attitude Toward Reading." *Reading Improvement* 39 (4): 186–95.

■ Chapter 7

Beck, I. L., M. G. McKeown, and L. Kucan. 2002. *Bringing Words to Life: Robust Vocabulary Instruction*. New York: Guilford.

Blachowicz, C., and P. Fisher. 2002. *Teaching Vocabulary in All Classrooms*. Upper Saddle River, NJ: Merrill Prentice Hall.

Brenner, G. A. 2003. *Webster's New World American Idioms Handbook*. Indianapolis, IN: Wiley.

Bromley, K. 2007. "Nine Things Every Teacher Should Know About Words and Vocabulary Instruction." *Journal of Adolescent and Adult Literacy* 50: 528–37.

Daintith, J. 2005. *A Dictionary of Science*. 5th ed. New York: Oxford University Press USA.

Dorling Kindersley. 2008. *Merriam-Webster Children's Dictionary*. London: Author.

Editors of the American Heritage Dictionaries. 2005. *The American Heritage Science Dictionary*. Boston: Houghton Mifflin.

Graves, M. F. 2006. *The Vocabulary Book: Learning and Instruction*. New York: Teachers College.

Langmuir, E., and N. Lynton. 2000. *The Yale Dictionary of Art and Artists*. New Haven, CT: Yale.

Marzano, R. 2004. *Building Background Knowledge for Academic Achievement*. Alexandria, VA: Association for Supervision and Curriculum Development.

Nelson, D. 2003. *The Penguin Dictionary of Mathematics*. 3d ed. New York: Penguin.

Root, B. 1993. *My First Dictionary: 1000 Words, Pictures, and Definitions*. London: Dorling Kindersley.

Spears, R. A. 2006. *American Slang Dictionary*. 4th ed. New York: McGraw-Hill.

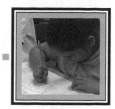

A Study Guide for *Learning Words Inside and Out*

This study guide is intended to support your understanding of the concepts presented in *Learning Words Inside and Out, Grades 1–6: Vocabulary Instruction That Boosts Achievement in All Subject Areas*, by Nancy Frey and Douglas Fisher.

You can use this study guide as you finish each chapter or after you complete the whole book. Prompts and questions are intended to promote personal reflection but could also be used to foster small-group discussions between colleagues.

CHAPTER

1

Why Teaching Subject Area Words Can Make or Break Achievement

1. Frey and Fisher talk about the unmet vocabulary needs of elementary students. Discuss several of the reasons for these unmet needs within the context of your own school.

2. Consider your own experiences with learning new words. How do you typically learn them? What are the implications for your classroom instruction?

3. Discuss the role word knowledge plays in writing.

4. Word knowledge is often described on a continuum of shallow to deep. Discuss the degrees of understanding that researchers like Dale, O'Rourke, and Bamman (1971) have described.

5. Discuss the differences between general, specialized, and technical words. Is it important to teach words from each of these categories? Why?

6. Frey and Fisher have developed an academic vocabulary model that consists of five big ideas. Following is a rubric that educators can use to evaluate how they are integrating these big ideas across the school day as part of a schoolwide initiative. Using the rubric, how might you describe the vocabulary efforts at your school?

Fostering a Schoolwide Vocabulary Initiative

How do students acquire and extend their academic vocabulary across the school day?					
	5	**4**	**3**	**2**	**1**
***Intentional Instruction:* Words are identified by subject and/or grade level**	Words are identified using a framework for selection. Word lists include general, specialized, and technical vocabulary and are shared across grade levels.	All grade levels select a range of general, specialized, and technical vocabulary by subject, but these are shared only within the grade level.	Some words are selected by grade level and subject, although these are driven by textbook lists (primarily technical vocabulary).	Individual teachers are applying a framework for selecting vocabulary, although these are not being shared outside the grade level.	Individual teachers are identifying words using the textbook (technical vocabulary), and these are not known to others in the grade level and school.
***Transparent Instruction:* Teacher modeling and think-alouds**	All teachers have received professional development in modeling and use it daily in their instruction. They share their practices with one another.	Some grade levels have received professional development in modeling and are using it daily.	All teachers have received professional development in modeling, but it is not yet being regularly implemented.	Individual teachers are sharing their modeling practices with one another through peer visits.	There are individual experts using teacher modeling, but there is no opportunity to share practices with others.
***Useable Instruction:* Peer talk and small-group collaboration**	Oral language practices are schoolwide and all teachers integrate peer talk and/or small-group collaboration daily.	Some grade levels use oral language daily and are emerging as skilled practitioners.	Some grade levels are planning ways to integrate peer talk and small-group collaboration into daily practice.	There are individual teachers who use peer talk and small-group collaboration, but there has not been an opportunity to work with others.	Instruction is dominated by whole-group lectures followed by silent, independent work.

continues on next page

How do students acquire and extend their academic vocabulary across the school day?					
	5	**4**	**3**	**2**	**1**
Personalized Instruction: **Independent and individual learning**	Students schoolwide consolidate their understanding through activities that promote spiral review and metacognition.	Grade levels are collaborating to build professional knowledge with colleagues.	Some grade levels have developed a plan for how students increase vocabulary metacognition and spiral review.	Individual teachers are becoming skilled at personalizing instruction, although there is no mechanism for sharing practice.	Independent work emphasizes isolated skills and memorization.
Prioritizing Vocabulary: **Words of the week and wide reading**	The school has implemented a plan and teachers receive regular professional development to refine practice.	The school has created a plan for schoolwide vocabulary and wide reading (sustained silent reading and independent reading).	The school has created a plan for either schoolwide vocabulary *or* wide reading.	The school is studying schoolwide vocabulary and wide reading for future planning.	There is no plan and no current initiative to examine these schoolwide practices.

Make It Intentional

A Framework for Daily Word Learning

1. Explain what *intentional vocabulary instruction* means. Why do the authors suggest that teachers should teach more than just words found in the classroom textbook?

2. Discuss the decision-making model that Frey and Fisher have developed for vocabulary selection. How might this model help you select words to teach in your own classroom?

3. How might a primary-grade teacher use the Dolch sight word list for vocabulary instruction? How could an intermediate-grade teacher use Coxhead's Academic Word List for similar purposes? How might Ogden's Basic English Word List help teachers of English learners?

4. In what ways would students benefit from learning about Latin and Greek root words, suffixes, and prefixes?

5. Discuss how subject area teachers might select technical vocabulary words to teach.

6. As mentioned in this chapter, teacher modeling can be an effective means by which to teach vocabulary alongside content instruction. How might you incorporate modeling, vocabulary instruction, and content teaching simultaneously in your classroom?

7. Why is collaboration between students important for academic vocabulary acquisition?

8. Frey and Fisher describe how teachers might use journal writing in mathematics to promote independent use of vocabulary words. What types of activities might you try in your content area? How might journal writing assignments advance vocabulary and concept understanding in other content areas?

Make It Transparent

Showing Students Your Thinking About Words

1. Why might a teacher explain his thinking when reading a piece of text? How could you use this strategy?

2. What does it mean to model context clues? Discuss the four categories for natural contexts that Beck, McKeown, and McCaslin (1983) developed.

3. What are the five ways in which context clues are provided by authors?

4. Frey and Fisher suggest that teachers devote time to modeling morphology and word parts. What prefixes, suffixes, root words, cognates, and word families might you teach in your content area?

5. How could a teacher model the use of resources when deciphering word meaning?

Make It Useable

Harnessing the Power of Peer Conversations

1. Discuss the research that supports the use of oral language to foster vocabulary development.

2. Explain the characteristics of effective peer learning. Develop a plan for incorporating these characteristics into a collaborative activity for your content area.

3. Consider the authors' three tips for successful peer interactions, and complete the following chart.

Applying the Tips for Successful Peer Interactions

Tip	What Does It Mean?	How Does It Apply to My Classroom?
Tip 1: Provide students with a purpose statement.		
Tip 2: Remember that variety is the spice of life.		
Tip 3: Integrate vocabulary activities into the content flow.		

4. Describe the use of partner and group discussions to help students clarify vocabulary understanding. What collaborative oral activities might you incorporate into your curriculum?

5. The use of student think-alouds and reciprocal teaching provides opportunities for students to talk about reading while clarifying vocabulary. Compare and contrast how these two strategies support vocabulary development.

6. Choose two or three graphic organizer structures from those described by Frey and Fisher. Describe how each might be suited to a certain topic in your content area.

7. Consider the following approaches for vocabulary development. Complete the chart.

Applying Various Approaches for Vocabulary Development

Strategy	What Is It?	How Could I Use It?
Semantic feature analysis		
Concept circles		
Shades of meaning		

8. How might you use written approaches to building academic vocabulary in your classroom? Discuss two or three possible strategies for doing this.

Make It Personal

Consolidating Students' Word Learning Through Individual Activities

1. Discuss the three characteristics of effective learners that Murdoch and Wilson (2006) have identified.

2. Nagy (1988) described three conditions needed for students to learn vocabulary: integration, repetition, and meaningful use. Explain what these three conditions mean in terms of word learning.

3. Review the various suggestions offered by the authors for consolidating individual learning through logs. Describe each strategy briefly, considering how each might apply to your grade level.

4. Complete the following chart for strategies that incorporate word manipulation to consolidate individual learning.

Applying Word-Manipulation Strategies

Stragegy for Manipulating Words	What Is It?	How Could I Use It?
Word sorts		
Word cards		
Mnemonics		

5. Generative sentences and writing frames can help students consolidate learning through composing. Explain how you might incorporate these two strategies into a subject that you teach.

6. Why do the authors recommend that assessment of academic vocabulary acquisition be carried out across teacher modeling, peer interaction, and individual learning?

Make It a Priority

Creating a Schoolwide Focus
on Learning Words

1. Explain how words of the week may be incorporated as a part of a schoolwide vocabulary effort. Is this a strategy that might work at your school?

2. Consider the discussion of word walls. How might you use a word wall in your classroom?

3. What is wide reading and how can it affect vocabulary development?

4. What role does student interest in a topic play in incidental vocabulary learning?

5. Discuss the components of an effective sustained silent reading (SSR) program as identified by Janice Pilgreen (2000). How might SSR be successfully implemented at your school or in your classroom? If there already is an effective SSR program, reflect on what makes it successful.

6. How might you incorporate independent reading into each content area of instruction? What types of reading materials would you suggest for students?

Make It Your Own

How to Keep Learning About
Academic Vocabulary

1. Summarize the five lessons Frey and Fisher learned. In what ways do these reflect your experiences?

2. Which types of resources for the classroom might you acquire to support your own professional learning about academic vocabulary instruction? What materials might you acquire to support student learning?

Index

Continued from p. iv